The[...]
From T[...]

On Everything And Anything Hollywood Loves To Talk About

SEX: "Is that a gun in your pocket or are you just pleased to see me?" (*She Done Him Wrong*)

MARRIAGE: "Marriage is like a dull meal, with the dessert at the beginning." (*Moulin Rouge*)

DEATH: "There are worse things in life than death. I mean, if you've ever spent an evening with an insurance salesman." (*Love and Death*)

SPORTS: "I'd never sleep with a player hittin' under .200 unless he had a lot of RBI's and was a great glove man up the middle." (*Bull Durham*)

POLITICS: "There may be honor among thieves, but there's none in politicians." (*Lawrence of Arabia*)

DRINKING: "She drove me to drink. That's the one thing I'm indebted to her for." (*Never Give a Sucker an Even Break*)

SHOW BUSINESS: "What he did to Shakespeare, we are doing now to Poland." (*To Be or Not to Be*)

"Etcetera, etcetera, etcetera."
(*The King and I*)

The Best Lines—
From The Best Movies—
On Everything And
Anything Hollywood
Loves To Talk About

I COULDA BEEN A CONTENDER

GERALD GARDNER

WARNER BOOKS

A Time Warner Company

WARNER BOOKS EDITION

Copyright © 1992 by Gerald Gardner
All rights reserved.

Cover design and illustration by Irving Freeman
Cover photographs from Wide World Photo

Warner Books, Inc.
1271 Avenue of the Americas
New York, NY 10020

 A Time Warner Company

Printed in the United States of America

First Printing: June, 1992

10 9 8 7 6 5 4 3 2 1

*To Lindsay Gardner
and Karen K. Gardner*

CONTENTS

INTRODUCTION

It is time we got back to the words.

Today, what draws us to the movies is special effects, car chases, movie stars, high-concept plots.

Not the words.

It used to be that speech was golden. In the plays of Shaw, Wilde, Tennessee Williams, Arthur Miller, Lillian Hellman, Edward Albee, Eugene O'Neill, William Saroyan, and Clifford Odets. The words would sing and snap with wit and emotion. All a playwright *had* were the words. He had to hold an audience for two hours with nothing but words. There was a set or two, costumes, lighting, and of course the actors. But words were the lure.

In the early years, the so-called Golden Years of Hollywood, the words were still important. There were giants writing the words in those days, like F. Scott Fitzgerald, William Faulkner, Ben Hecht, Herman Mankiewicz, George S. Kaufman, Marc Connelly, Nathanael West, S.J. Perelman, Preston Sturges, Dorothy Parker, Arthur Kober, John O'Hara, Donald Ogden Stewart, Samson Raphaelson, Gene Fowler, and Nunnally Johnson. There were writers like Raymond Chandler, Anita Luce, Ring Lardner, and Moss Hart. There were famous playwrights like Philip

Barry, S.N. Behrman, Maxwell Anderson, Robert E. Sherwood, and Sidney Howard.

Oh, yes, the writers all felt it was a prostitution of their talents, but it was a joyous prostitution. And using their convivial relationship with other great writers—people who loved the words—they lured their peers to Hollywood with promises of money and fun. Their colleagues were laboring for little money on the East Coast, writing the words for newspapers, magazines, and the theater. When they all came west they fell in love with the movies that corrupted and demeaned them. The burnt children loved the fire. For they were writing good words. They suffered compromise, self-delusion, and were distracted by money. And a third of them became alcoholics. But they had the joy of writing wonderful, witty, expressive words. Comedy, drama, adventure, romance, epics. The works.

Yes, they suffered from neglect. There was the tyrannical contract system. There was the blacklist. And they were ignored by the critics and the historians. It seems the *directors* deserved the homage. It was their vision, their personal signatures on the films, not the writers. Were there really writers? Didn't the actors make up the words as they went along? The films were those of John Ford; the words of Dudley Nichols got barely a footnote. It was the Capra Touch, not the words of Robert Risken.

Today, if a screenwriter gets any attention, between the eye-popping special effects, it is Woody Allen, William Goldman, Robert Towne—the bankable, deal-making hyphenates. They are not just writers; they are writer-directors or writer-producers. They have power.

Movie writers have no power. They have nothing but their words.

* * *

Here are some of the words.

In this compendium of lines from motion pictures, there are words that sparkle with humor and wisdom and wit. Where would the directors or the stars be without them?

A great many of these words are from recent movies. Thankfully, there are still some movies where a glistening arrangement of words escapes the revisions of the stars and the studios—often because the man who wrote them is also the director who sees to it they are performed as written. But often because they are so riveting that they demand to be heard over the pounding music and the special effects and the sound of crashing metal.

But a great many of the words are from the movies of the thirties and the forties. The reason there are so many fine lines from that era is that those films were controlled by the producers—producers who recognized good writing. Men like Irving Thalberg, Darryl Zanuck, and Hal Wallis. Good producers respected good scripts. As the directors took charge of the films and the scripts, literacy took a back seat to the mood, the performance, and the crash cuts. As the prestige of the directors rose, concern for the sparkling words declined.

This is doubtless hyperbole. Look at the screenplays of Francis Coppola, of Woody Allen, of James Brooks, of Billy Wilder and John Huston—but notice that all these men direct their own works.

So before we return to the local cineplex to watch the high-tech magic of ''Terminator 3'' or the vivid colors of the next ''Dick Tracy,'' let us wallow in the splendor of words . . . words well written, words well spoken, words that evoke a scene, a star, a film, an era.

Words, words, words.

CHAPTER ONE

★

Classic Lines

They are not words full of wisdom and wit. They are not epigrams that explode in the mind like bits of truth and irony. But they are the most memorable lines in half a century of movie going. If you have any doubt of how precious words are in the movies, look at these famous lines from the cinema. In popular music they call them standards. On the stage they are the classics. In books they are the bestsellers. These lines have become part of the lexicon. We use these phrases and combinations of words as we use the basic nouns and verbs of the language. Generally, they come from the most popular films, like "The Wizard of Oz," "Casablanca," "Love Story," "All About Eve," "Chinatown," "Gone With the Wind," "Now, Voyager" and "The Jazz Singer." But on occasion, their genesis is a film that we do not remember at all, only the line. After all, the famous line, "Yonda is dah castle of my fodda," spoken by Tony Curtis, originated in a forgettable film called "The Black Shield of Falmouth." If screenwriters could collect a royalty whenever someone used these classic lines, these lines that have infiltrated our everyday speech, they could retire from their oblivion and their humiliation.

"Fasten your seat belt, it's going to be a bumpy night."
ALL ABOUT EVE

"It's even better when you help."
TO HAVE AND HAVE NOT

"Love means never having to say you're sorry."
LOVE STORY

"They call me *Mr*. Tibbs."
IN THE HEAT OF THE NIGHT

"If you want to call me that, smile."
THE VIRGINIAN

"I've a feeling we're not in Kansas anymore."
THE WIZARD OF OZ

"You ain't heard nothin' yet!"
THE JAZZ SINGER

"Go ahead, make my day."
DIRTY HARRY

"The Calla lilies are in bloom again."
STAGE DOOR

"Another nice mess you got us into."
WAY OUT WEST

"She's my sister . . . she's my daughter . . ."
CHINATOWN

"Here's looking at you, kid."
CASABLANCA

"Frankly, my dear, I don't give a damn."
GONE WITH THE WIND

"We want to be alone."
NINOTCHKA

"Me Tarzan, you Jane."
TARZAN THE APE MAN

"My name is Bond. James Bond."
GOLDFINGER

"Read my lips."
MAGNUM FORCE

"Shane! Come back! Shane!"

SHANE

"Buelah, peel me a grape."

I'M NO ANGEL

"This man was once important. Attention must be paid."

DEATH OF A SALESMAN

"The rain in Spain stays mainly in the plain."

MY FAIR LADY

"Play 'Misty' for me."

PLAY MISTY FOR ME

"I'm gonna make him an offer he can't refuse."

THE GODFATHER

"I'm ready for my closeup, Mr. De Mille."

SUNSET BOULEVARD

"You're going out a youngster but you've got to come back a star."

42ND STREET

"We rob banks."

BONNIE AND CLYDE

"It's the stuff that dreams are made of."

THE MALTESE FALCON

"Oh, Jerry, don't let's ask for the moon. We have the stars."

NOW, VOYAGER

"I coulda been a contender."

ON THE WATERFRONT

"I'll think about it tomorrow."

GONE WITH THE WIND

"I have always depended on the kindness of strangers."

A STREETCAR NAMED DESIRE

"I'm mad as hell and I'm not going to take this anymore."

NETWORK

"I'm a ba-a-a-ad boy!"

ABBOTT AND COSTELLO MEET FRANKENSTEIN

"May the force be with you."

STAR WARS

"He-ee-ee-ere's Johnny."

THE SHINING

"But first and foremost, I remember Mama."

I REMEMBER MAMA

"What do you feel like doing tonight?"
"I don't know, Ange. What do *you* feel like doing?"

MARTY

CHAPTER TWO

★

Sex and Sin

Words about sex have always been the mainstay of the popular arts. This posed something of a problem to the screenwriters, since for over forty years—from 1925 to 1968—the Hays Office, Hollywood's outrageous self-censorship agency, carefully eliminated from movie scripts any line that touched on sexual subjects. All the sex ended up on the cutting room floor. When the lines dealt with copulation, adultery, prostitution, homosexuality, seduction, nudity, vulgarity, blasphemy, sodomy, or rape, the words were taboo. Nevertheless, screenwriters managed to slide past the bluenoses a small compendium of lines on matters sexual. Once the Hays Office was abolished, of course, the door was open to more candid sexual dialogue, but somehow with the removal of the taboos, the lines were less delicious: when you are old enough to reach the cookie jar, the taste for cookies has left you. Certain writers are especially adept at writing memorable sexual dialogue—writers like Woody Allen, in films like "Love and Death," "Bananas," and "Annie Hall." George Axelrod wrote some memorable lines in "Will Success Spoil Rock Hunter?"; Buck Henry added some salacious wit to "The Graduate." Some screenplays erupt with explosively sexual comedy lines, as in Dudley Moore's scene with the prostitute in "Arthur," and George Segal's lines with his mother in "Where's Poppa?" Back in the thirties, even the well-upholstered Mae West slipped some sexual lines past the Legion of Decency in "She Done Him Wrong" and "She's No Angel," until the Hearst press drove her out of the movie business. Naturally, an occasional Tennessee Williams line about sex and depravity crept past the censors and into "Cat on a Hot Tin Roof" and "The Night of the Iguana." Here then is a compendium of memorable sexual lines that the censors failed to excise, or lines that were written once the censors were history.

"Jewish women don't believe in sex after marriage."

LOVE AND DEATH

"Mrs. Robinson, you're trying to seduce me."

THE GRADUATE

"The only question I've ever asked any woman is what time is your husband comin' home."

HUD

"Do you want a leg or a breast?"

TO CATCH A THIEF

"I like to watch."

BEING THERE

"Some men are paying two hundred dollars for me and here you are turning down a freebee."

KLUTE

"When I was fourteen I knew I should carry around an emergency contraceptive. By the time I got to use it, it was dust."

ANNIE HALL

"The coat came first, then the tie, then the shirt.
Now, according to Hoyle, after that the pants should be
next . . ."

IT HAPPENED ONE NIGHT

"How about coming up to my place for a spot of heavy
breathing?"

PETE 'N' TILLY

"You can't make love on wet sand . . . it just gets into
everything."

WILL SUCCESS SPOIL ROCK HUNTER?

"Slowly, slowly. Against the beat."

BLOWUP

"You'll never learn. You'll be a eunuch all your life."

A FUNNY THING HAPPENED ON THE WAY TO THE FORUM

"Adam and Eve are in the Garden of Eden and he says:
'Stand back! I don't know how big this thing gets.' "

PUNCHLINE

"I don't know if you're a detective or a pervert."

BLUE VELVET

"You mean Dad used to do it!"

BRIGHTON BEACH MEMOIRS

"So is somebody goin' to go to bed with somebody or
what?"

BULL DURHAM

"Do I have 'fuck me' written on my forehead?"

COCKTAIL
woman to forward bartender

"Well, Howard, it all went by so fast, I just had no
idea that it would be so quick."

BANANAS
honeymooner to Howard Cosell

"It was Henry James, wasn't it? *My Sexual Problem* by
Henry James. Sequel to 'The Turn of the Screw.' "

ANNIE HALL

"If you're going to be the little brother of Mary, you must remember that your body is your most dangerous enemy."

THE DEVIL'S PLAYGROUND
instructions at a seminary

"I looked for you in my closet tonight."

BLUE VELVET

"That looks to me like two elephants making love to a men's glee club."

TAKE THE MONEY AND RUN
taking inkblot test

"Is this your first rape?"

WHERE'S POPPA?

"Is that a gun in your pocket or are you just pleased to see me?"

SHE DONE HIM WRONG

"Any time you got nothing to do—and lots of time to do it—come on up."

SHE DONE HIM WRONG

"First we'll have an orgy and then we'll see Tony Bennett."

BOB AND CAROL AND TED AND ALICE

"The psychiatrist asked me if I thought sex was dirty and I said it is if you're doing it right."

TAKE THE MONEY AND RUN

"It's just a shame that a man with his talents didn't become an obstetrician."

CACTUS FLOWER

"Are you frightened by the word *rape*? All women love a man of spirit."

TOM JONES

"Years from now, when you talk about this—and you will—be kind."

TEA AND SYMPATHY

"My mother told me never to enter any man's room in months ending in *R*."

LOVE AFFAIR

"He's been reading *God's Little Acre* for over a year now. He's underlined every erotic passage and added exclamation points—and after a certain pornographic climax, he's inserted the words 'well written.' "

MISTER ROBERTS

"Men are usually so bored with virgins. I'm so glad you're not."

THE MOON IS BLUE

"Good heavens, Agnes! You have a bust. Where have you been hiding it all these years?"

MAME

"I've reached that realistic age when I have to choose between having fun and a heart attack."

THE GRASSHOPPER

"This may come as a shock to you, but there are some men who don't end every sentence with a proposition."

PILLOW TALK

"He looks as if he knows what I look like without my shimmy."

GONE WITH THE WIND

" 'Very nice' is hardly the phrase to describe two bodies locked in heavenly transport . . . 'Very nice' is when you get a get-well card from your butcher."

A TOUCH OF CLASS

"Did he tell you about the time he overwhelmed a forty-five-year-old maiden by the simple tactic of being the first man in her life to ask her a direct question?"

MISTER ROBERTS

"Well, I'll tell you the truth now. I ain't a real cowboy, but I am one helluva stud."

MIDNIGHT COWBOY

"Goodness, what beautiful diamonds."
"Goodness had nothing to do with it."

NIGHT AFTER NIGHT

"Oh, Big Daddy, you don't think I ravaged a football
hero!"

CAT ON A HOT TIN ROOF

"Sooner or later, the innocence of your daughter cannot
be respected if the family is going to continue."

THE ROSE TATTOO

"The only people who make love all the time are
liars."

GIGI

"She was giving me the kind of look I could feel in my
hip pocket."

FAREWELL, MY LOVELY

"Why don't you come up sometime 'n see me. . . ."

SHE DONE HIM WRONG

"You got nothing to worry about: the walls of Jericho
will protect you from the big bad wolf."

IT HAPPENED ONE NIGHT

"Nature, Mr. Allnut, is what we are put into this world
to rise above."

THE AFRICAN QUEEN

"Don't you think it's better for a girl to be preoccupied
with sex than occupied?"

THE MOON IS BLUE

"Come on, darling. Why don't you kick off your
spurs?"

GIANT

"If it didn't take men to make babies I wouldn't have
anything to do with any of you."

LONELY ARE THE BRAVE

"There are worse things than chastity. . . ."
"Yes—lunacy and death."

THE NIGHT OF THE IGUANA

"I'm in spasm."

A TOUCH OF CLASS

"Come on, Charley. You wanna do it? Let's do it, right here on the Oriental."

PRIZZI'S HONOR

"I've arrived at the age where a platonic friendship can be sustained on the highest moral plane."

LIMELIGHT

"I think he's upset. We didn't order enough."
"Shall we cheer him up? Waiter! Do you have any rooms?"

A MAN AND A WOMAN

"If this is foreplay, I'm a dead man."

COCOON

"I make it a policy never to have sex before the first date."

SURRENDER

"Are you a hooker? Jesus, I forgot. I just thought I was doing great with you."

ARTHUR

"Well, I don't know how to put it—but I have this thing about girls."

SOME LIKE IT HOT

"I like the lights *on*."
"Then go home and turn them on."

TERMS OF ENDEARMENT

"Going to a man's apartment always ends in one of two ways: Either a girl is willing to lose her virtue, or she fights for it. I don't want to lose mine, and I think it's vulgar to fight for it. . . ."

THE MOON IS BLUE

"She'd sleep with a snake if you held its head."
HANNAH AND HER SISTERS

"That was the most fun I've had without laughing."
ANNIE HALL

"You mean you never enjoyed sex?"
"What's to enjoy? Love isn't physical. Love is spiritual. Like the great love that Ingrid Bergman had for Bing Crosby in 'The Bells of St. Mary's'. . . ."
LOVERS AND OTHER STRANGERS

"Small college and all. Musical beds is the faculty sport around here."
WHO'S AFRAID OF VIRGINIA WOOLF?

"He's like a spider and he expects me to redecorate his web."
PILLOW TALK

"I stayed at a hotel called the Tarantula Arms. . . . That's where I brought my victims."
A STREETCAR NAMED DESIRE

"I don't believe in jealousy. It's dumb. One thing though. Touch his dick and he's dead."
A FISH CALLED WANDA

"You should wear break-away clothes like the basketball players. . . ."
HANNAH AND HER SISTERS

"Here we are: middle-aged man reaffirming his middle-aged manhood and terrified young woman with a father complex."
NETWORK

"You know, it takes two to get one in trouble."
SHE DONE HIM WRONG

"You can either watch me or join me. One of them's more fun."
MY FAVORITE YEAR

"Through the window? That's a funny way for a cousin to leave."

THE BAREFOOT CONTESSA

"Your idea of fidelity is not having more than one man in the bed at the same time."

DARLING

"Don't knock masturbation. It's sex with someone I love."

ANNIE HALL

CHAPTER
THREE

★

Philosophy and
Wisdom

When we look for cogent expressions of philosophy and wisdom, we are not apt to seek them in movie screenplays. We are accustomed to finding epigrammatic expressions of wisdom in *Bartlett's Quotations*, or the collected epigrams of Oscar Wilde or Bernard Shaw. Yet surprisingly, movie screenplays yield a rich lode of these philosophical cogencies. Screenwriters are more concerned with the *motion* in motion pictures, the movement of actors, the narrative flow of action, the delineation of character. They have scant time to put words in their characters' mouths with which they reflect on the nature of life. If they do, they should be writing essays for the *Atlantic Monthly*. At two thousand dollars a week, screenwriters are expected to keep the ball rolling. If they pause to reflect, it should be in a dressing-room mirror. Yet movie scribes are often serious men and women. They are deep (though deep down they are said to be shallow). We find numerous philosophic thoughts well expressed in the words of Woody Allen (especially in "Love and Death" and "Hannah and Her Sisters"). Oscar Wilde's novel "The Picture of Dorian Gray" was a cornucopia of epigrams and many of them survived in George Sanders's dialogue in the movie version. Bill Goldman's film adaptation of his play "The Lion in Winter" is rich with wry observations on the battles of parents and children. Movies as disparate as "Citizen Kane" and "Bull Durham" are rich in lines that are as thoughtful as they are witty. Occasionally, it seems, a screenwriter will invent a reflective character for the sole purpose of making him a spokesman for the writer's philosophic thoughts. Here are some of the musings that screenwriters have slipped into their dialogue.

"He who hesitates is poor."

THE PRODUCERS

"People who are beautiful make their own laws."

THE ROMAN SPRING OF MRS. STONE

"The wise man shall be delivered into the hands of his enemies whether they can pay the delivery charges or not."

LOVE AND DEATH

"Words with a *K* in it are funny. You didn't know that, did you?"

THE SUNSHINE BOYS

"Some people take and some people get took."

THE APARTMENT

"Money is like fertilizer. It does more good if you spread it around."

HELLO, DOLLY!

"Only cream and bastards rise."

HARPER

"A good influence is the worst influence of all."

THE PICTURE OF DORIAN GRAY

"Good manners spoils good food."

INDISCREET

"A man who's too afraid to die's too afraid to live."

THE MISFITS

"Never fall in love during a total eclipse."

A FUNNY THING HAPPENED ON THE WAY TO THE FORUM

"A man is what he does; a woman is what she is."

THE MEN

"Nothing's easy, is it?"
"Nothing good."

THE BEST MAN

"The world is made for people who aren't first in self-awareness."

BULL DURHAM

"This contempt for money is just another trick of the rich to keep the poor without it."

GODFATHER II

"Human beings are divided into mind and body. The mind embraces all the nobler aspirations like poetry and philosophy. But the body has all the fun."

LOVE AND DEATH

"Sticks and stones may break my bones, but words cause permanent damage."

TALK RADIO

"Talk is overrated as a means of resolving disputes."

COCKTAIL

"The trouble with ambitious men is that they aren't ready to do what's necessary."

BODY HEAT

"There's what's right and there's what's right and never the twain shall meet."

RAISING ARIZONA

"Money won is twice as sweet as money earned."

THE COLOR OF MONEY

"The only thing that gives orders in this world is balls."

SCARFACE

"The past is a foreign country. They do things differently there."

THE GO-BETWEEN

"California—I can't live in any city where the only cultural advantage is that you can make a right turn on a red light."

ANNIE HALL

"Things change."

THINGS CHANGE

"In a world where carpenters get resurrected, anything is possible."

THE LION IN WINTER

"It's all addition and subtraction: the rest is conversation."

FORCE OF EVIL

"I'll think about it tomorrow."

GONE WITH THE WIND

"Dirty old men seem to get away with a lot more."

BAREFOOT IN THE PARK

"It's the innocents who get slaughtered."

THE SPY WHO CAME IN FROM THE COLD

"The ends justify the means, eh? Let me tell you—there are no ends, just means."

THE BEST MAN

"If it turns out that there *is* a God, I don't think that He's evil. I think the worst thing you can say about Him is that He's probably an underachiever."

LOVE AND DEATH

"Everything I like to do is either illegal, immoral, or fattening."

NEVER GIVE A SUCKER AN EVEN BREAK

"I always say the law was meant to be interpreted in a lenient manner."

HUD

"Everything ends badly, otherwise it wouldn't end."

COCKTAIL

"Tall people are very nervous. Too far from the earth."

BLAZING SADDLES

"If the headline is big enough, it *makes* the news big enough."

CITIZEN KANE

"Everybody knows everybody is dying. That's why people are as good as they are."

BANG THE DRUM SLOWLY

"You can stay here for nothing."
"Nothing is sometimes too much."

RICHARD'S THINGS

"Popular? Nixon was popular. Hula hoops were popular. An epidemic of typhus is popular. Quantity doesn't imply quality."

ANNIE HALL

"There's a lot to be said for making people laugh . . . Did you know that's all some people have?"

SULLIVAN'S TRAVELS

"He that abideth in truth . . . shall dwell in the house of the Lord for six months with an option to buy."

LOVE AND DEATH

"Did it ever occur to you that some people are all repentance and no sin?"

GUYS AND DOLLS

"My life, when it is written, will read better than it lived."

THE LION IN WINTER

"How come in former lifetimes, everybody's somebody famous?"

BULL DURHAM

"The Sicilian people say—a big man knows the value of a small coin."

THINGS CHANGE

"*Carpe diem* . . . seize the day."

DEAD POETS SOCIETY

"I really wanted to be an anarchist but I didn't know where to go to register."

ANNIE HALL

"This is how society lives, halfway between the apes and the angels, aspiring to go up yet coming from down there."

GREYSTOKE: THE LEGEND OF TARZAN

"The more you drive, the less intelligent you are."

REPO MAN

"I've snapped and plotted all my life. There's no other way to be a king, alive, and fifty all at once."

THE LION IN WINTER

"The police are to society what dreams are to the individual."

FIRST NAME: CARMEN

"The hard truth is that the hungrier we get the more we need our heroes . . ."

THIS LAND IS MINE

"I believe we live two lives—the lives we learn with and the lives we live with after that."

THE NATURAL

"My father taught me—keep your friends close but your enemies closer."

GODFATHER II

"The powerful play goes on, and you may contribute a verse. What will your verse be?"

DEAD POETS SOCIETY

"Work hard, take chances, be very bold."

JULIA

"Health is the most important quality for man besides character."

HEALTH

"Good health is the most important thing, more than success, more than money, more than power."

GODFATHER II

"If your head says one thing and your whole life says another, your head always loses."

KEY LARGO

"A strong man needs a weak people. A strong people don't need a strong man."

VIVA ZAPATA!

"Play make man think. Thought make man wise. Wisdom make life endurable."

THE TEAHOUSE OF THE AUGUST MOON

"It's only fame, Lily. It's just a paint job. Just remember, it doesn't have anything to do with writing."

JULIA

"I proved once and for all the limb is mightier than the thumb."

IT HAPPENED ONE NIGHT
after stopping a car by
exposing her leg

"Cold are the hands of time that creep along relentlessly. . . . Alone our memories resist the disintegration . . . That's hard to say with false teeth."

THE PALM BEACH STORY

"The love of a man for a woman waxes and wanes like the moon, but the love of a brother is steadfast as the stars . . ."

BEAU GESTE

"The only men on earth worth their time on earth were the men who would fight for other men."

WATCH ON THE RHINE

"People say money talks, but between you and me, money keeps a secret better than anyone I know."

ONE GOOD COP

"I have a very pessimistic view of life . . . I feel that life is divided into the horrible and the miserable."

ANNIE HALL

"Hearts will never be practical until they can be made unbreakable."

THE WIZARD OF OZ

"I never answer letters from large organizations."

A THOUSAND CLOWNS

"The joy of giving is indeed a pleasure—especially when you get rid of something you don't want."

GOING MY WAY

"It's sort of a cause. I want everybody to be smart. . . . A world full of ignorant people is too dangerous to live in."

BORN YESTERDAY

"Corpulence makes a man reasonable, pleasant, and phlegmatic. Have you noticed that the nastiest of talents are invariably thin?"

SPARTACUS

"It's not enough that you have talent. You gotta have character, too . . . I sure got character now. I picked it up in a hotel room in Louisville."

THE HUSTLER

"A brave man is afraid of a lion three times: when he first sees its track, when he first hears its roar, and when he first looks it in the eye."

THE MACOMBER AFFAIR

"A starved body has a skinny soul."

VIVA ZAPATA!

"With enough courage, you can do without a reputation."

GONE WITH THE WIND

"Try to remember that, though ignorance becomes a southern gentleman, cowardice does not."

ANOTHER PART OF THE FOREST

"That's one of the tragedies of this life—that the men who are most in need of a beating-up are always enormous."

THE PALM BEACH STORY

"The earth was made round so we would not see too far down the road."

OUT OF AFRICA

"A coward I am, but I will hold your coat."

HOW GREEN WAS MY VALLEY

" 'Hurry' is the curse of civilization."

THE CHALK GARDEN

"Gold don't carry no curse with it. It all depends on whether or not the guy who finds it is the right guy."

THE TREASURE OF THE SIERRA MADRE

"People who hate the light usually hate the truth."

SEPARATE TABLES

"The only difference in men is the color of their neckties."

TOP HAT

"In Rome, dignity shortens life even more surely than disease."

SPARTACUS

"Dogs like us, we ain't such dogs as we think we are."

MARTY

"It's the duty of a newspaper to comfort the afflicted and to flick the comfortable."

INHERIT THE WIND

"There is an old Chinese proverb: 'Do not wake a sleeping tiger.'"

"Certainly not in a small boat."

LOVE IS A MANY-SPLENDORED THING

"Darwin was wrong. Man's still an ape."

INHERIT THE WIND

"If God ever wanted to be a fish, he'd be a whale."

MOBY DICK

"Don't look for happiness . . . it'll only make you miserable."

LOVERS AND OTHER STRANGERS

"I'll do my best to help you with your garden—and with the children. Their problems are similar."

THE CHALK GARDEN

"Your ignorance, brother, as the great Milton says, almost subdues my patience."

TOM JONES

"Ingenuity is never a substitute for intelligence."

THE MASK OF DIMITRIOS

"A man who tells lies merely hides the truth, but a man who tells half-lies has forgotten where he put it."

LAWRENCE OF ARABIA

"The history of the world proves that truth has no bearing on anything."

THE ICEMAN COMETH

"Life's never quite interesting enough, somehow. You people who come to the movies know that."

THE MATCHMAKER

"I don't have a lifestyle. I have a life."

CALIFORNIA SUITE

"To life! To the magnificent, dangerous, brief, brief, wonderful life and the courage to live it."

GRAND HOTEL

"Life is a banquet and most poor suckers are starving to death."

AUNTIE MAME

"What the gods give, they quickly take away. Time is jealous of you, Mr. Gray."

THE PICTURE OF DORIAN GRAY

"A life that is planned is a closed life . . . it can be endured perhaps. It cannot be lived."

THE INN OF THE SIXTH HAPPINESS

"Nobody ever lies about being lonely."

FROM HERE TO ETERNITY

"We're all on the outside of other people's lives, looking in."

POSSESSED

"You know what luck is? Luck is believing you're lucky . . ."

A STREETCAR NAMED DESIRE

"You may as well go to perdition in ermine. You're sure to come back in rags."

STAGE DOOR

"There are three things that men respect: the lash that descends, the yoke that breaks, and the sword that slays."

THE THIEF OF BAGDAD

"Chivalry is not only dead, it's decomposing."

THE PALM BEACH STORY

"I adore simple pleasures. They're the last refuge of the complex."

THE PICTURE OF DORIAN GRAY

"Never apologize and never explain—it's a sign of weakness."

SHE WORE A YELLOW RIBBON

"Even vultures have to eat."

THE CHILDREN'S HOUR

"Why did God give us hands? To grab. Well, grab!"
ZORBA THE GREEK

"God always has another custard pie up his sleeve."
GEORGY GIRL

"Oh, Richard, it profits a man nothing to give his soul for the whole world—but for Wales?"
A MAN FOR ALL SEASONS

"Live! Otherwise you got nothing to talk about in the locker room."
HAROLD AND MAUDE

"I've distilled everything to one simple principle—win or die."
DANGEROUS LIAISONS

"Men don't get smarter when they grow older. They just lose their hair."
THE PALM BEACH STORY

"Most people get by on a sort of creeping common sense and discover too late that the only things one never regrets are one's mistakes."
THE PICTURE OF DORIAN GRAY

"Man is the only animal that blushes—or needs to."
THE ADVENTURES OF MARK TWAIN

"You can be wrong without money but you can't be old without it."
CAT ON A HOT TIN ROOF

"Money talks, they say. All it ever said to me was 'good-bye.' "
NONE BUT THE LONELY HEART

"Sentiment has no cash value."
WE'RE NO ANGELS

"I like persons better than principles. A person with no principles is better than anything else in the world."
THE PICTURE OF DORIAN GRAY

"The German people love to sing, no matter what the situation."

<small>JUDGMENT AT NUREMBERG</small>

"Never say never."

<small>THE LONG, HOT SUMMER</small>

"A relationship is like a shark . . . it has to constantly move forward or it dies, and I think what we got on our hands is a dead shark."

<small>ANNIE HALL</small>

"There's no such thing as a good influence, Mr. Gray. All influence is immoral."

<small>THE PICTURE OF DORIAN GRAY</small>

"El Paso and Amarillo ain't no different than Sodom and Gomorrah—on a smaller scale, of course."

<small>DUEL IN THE SUN</small>

"It's very sad when you get old . . . Life is like a giant 'so what.' "

<small>HANNAH AND HER SISTERS</small>

"Once I tried to let a smile be my umbrella. I got awful wet."

<small>GENTLEMEN'S AGREEMENT</small>

"A son is a poor substitute for a lover."

<small>PSYCHO</small>

"If only the picture could change and I could be always what I am now. For that I would give everything . . ."

<small>THE PICTURE OF DORIAN GRAY</small>

"A fella ain't got a soul of his own, just a little piece of a big soul—the one big soul that belongs to ever'body."

<small>THE GRAPES OF WRATH</small>

"Good and evil are so close they are chained together in the soul."

<small>DR. JEKYLL AND MR. HYDE</small>

"I was thrown out of NYU my freshman year for cheating on my metaphysics final . . . I looked into the soul of the boy sitting next to me."

ANNIE HALL

"A weak mind isn't strong enough to hurt itself. Stupidity has saved many a man from going mad."

STAIRWAY TO HEAVEN

"The reason they can never answer the question: How could [the holocaust] actually happen? is that it's the wrong question. Given what people are, the question is: Why doesn't it happen more often?"

HANNAH AND HER SISTERS

"Tears wash the eyes that one can see better."

SHIP OF FOOLS

"Time, time. What is time? Swiss manufacture it. French hoard it. Italians want it. Americans say it is money. Hindus say it doesn't exist."

BEAT THE DEVIL

"Time ain't so important . . . seems like the longer I live, the more there is of it."

JEZEBEL

"A man sentenced to life can always 'spare a few minutes.' "

WE'RE NO ANGELS

"Opportunity's only got one hair on its head and you got to grab it while it's going by."

HAIL THE CONQUERING HERO

"When a man says he has exhausted life, you may be sure life has exhausted him."

THE PICTURE OF DORIAN GRAY

"Every man has his own sack of rocks to carry."

THE DARK AT THE TOP OF THE STAIRS

"Never trust anyone who functions from noble motives because they're never sure, and in the end, they'll let you down."

ANASTASIA

"No mob ever wants justice. They want vengeance."

QUO VADIS

"The Reverend Mother always says when the Lord closes a door somewhere he opens a window."

THE SOUND OF MUSIC

"If I ever acquire wisdom, I suppose I'll be wise enough to know what to do with it."

THE RAZOR'S EDGE

"What's the use of worrying? It's silly to worry, isn't it? You're gone today and here tomorrow."

THE COCOANUTS

"Jews know two things: suffering and where to find great Chinese food."

MY FAVORITE YEAR

"Intellectuals are like the Mafia. They only kill their own."

STARDUST MEMORIES

"Nietzsche . . . said that the life we live we're going to live over and over again the exact same way for eternity. Great. That means I'll have to sit through the Ice Capades again."

HANNAH AND HER SISTERS

"When the legend becomes a fact, print the legend."

THE MAN WHO SHOT LIBERTY VALANCE

"The best thing about the past is you figure out what it was that could have made you happy."

LOVERS AND OTHER STRANGERS

"No civilized man ever regrets a pleasure, and no uncivilized man ever knows what a pleasure is."

THE PICTURE OF DORIAN GRAY

"As you grow older, you'll find that the only things you regret are the things you didn't do."

MILDRED PIERCE

"A generous man is merely a fool in the eyes of a thief."

TOM JONES

"If you give a hungry man a loaf of bread, that's democracy. If you leave the wrapper on it, it's imperialism."

A FOREIGN AFFAIR

"Life, every now and then, behaves as if it has seen too many bad movies . . ."

THE BAREFOOT CONTESSA

CHAPTER
FOUR

★

Put-Downs and
Insults

S ome people build a reputation as curmudgeons on their ability to insult others. We think of George S. Kaufman, Dorothy Parker, George Jean Nathan, H.L. Mencken, Alexander Woolcott, Cleveland Amory, Calvin Trillin, and Fran Lebowitz. Yet a close reading of America's screenplays reveals a rich compendium of put-downs and sour notes. Given the frustrations and humiliations of the screenwriting trade (Jack Warner called writers "schmucks with Underwoods") it is not surprising that Hollywood writers were prolific in producing seething put-downs. Undoubtedly, the screenwriters pictured themselves saying these withering lines to Harry Cohn and Louis B. Mayer. These lines could most reliably be put into the mouths of such actors as Thelma Ritter, W.C. Fields, Clifton Webb, Oscar Levant, and the inimitable Groucho. Neil Simon's original movies, and the adaptations of his stage hits, are studded with marvelous put-downs. Simon's secret is to fill every scene with conflict, for conflict breeds insults and witty affronts. Screenwriters have put clever insults in the mouths of courtesans, harridans, law professors, Broadway columnists, debutantes, presidents, kings, publishers, theatrical producers, doctors, composers, and female commissars. This compendium makes a fine resource for the splenetic reader.

"You're not too smart, are you? I like that in a man."
BODY HEAT

"You're a cookie full of arsenic."
SWEET SMELL OF SUCCESS

"Will ya do me a favor, Harry? Drop dead."
BORN YESTERDAY

"You are not a person, you are an experience."
A THOUSAND CLOWNS

"Do you have a dime, Mr. Hart? Go and phone your mother and tell her you will never be a lawyer."
THE PAPER CHASE

"He wears a seat belt in a drive-in movie."
THE ODD COUPLE

"Not smuck—schmuck!"
ISHTAR

"He has all the character of a dog except loyalty."
THE BEST MAN

"Perhaps you ought to stay with relatives, distant relatives."
A FUNNY THING HAPPENED ON THE WAY TO THE FORUM

"He used to be a yes-man but he got himself some guts and now he goes around bravely saying 'maybe' to everybody."
A THOUSAND CLOWNS

"What beat me?"
"Character."
THE HUSTLER

"What a dump!"
BEYOND THE FOREST

"You want to do me a really big favor? Smoke toward New Jersey."

THE ODD COUPLE

"Did you know he was once locked in the john overnight? He wrote out his entire will on a half a roll of toilet paper."

THE ODD COUPLE

"He's the only man in the world with clenched hair."

THE ODD COUPLE

"You probably think I'm silly."
"Yes, I'm afraid I do."

SWING TIME

"I'm sorry—I'm anal."
"That's the polite word for what you are."

ANNIE HALL

"This . . . this . . . swishbuckler!"

ZORRO, THE GAY BLADE

"You—you cossack!"

SWING TIME
debutante to policeman

"You mutinous dogs!"

MUTINY ON THE BOUNTY

"He's got an empty stomach and it's gone to his head."

SOME LIKE IT HOT

"He had no conception of the cello. He was blowing into it."

TAKE THE MONEY AND RUN

"That's the second sentence you've started with 'I.' "

CITIZEN KANE

"I'll bet she wears corrective hats."

CACTUS FLOWER

"The only school that's accepted Flap is in Des Moines."
"He can't even do the simple things—like fail locally."
TERMS OF ENDEARMENT

"You are so self-righteous. . . . You think you're God!"
"I've gotta model myself after *someone*."
MANHATTAN

"He's giving me the finger."
THE SUNSHINE BOYS

"I like the way you manage to state the obvious with such a sense of discovery."
THE BEST MAN

"I want to watch the two of you go picnicking on each other. You have a gift for hating."
THE LION IN WINTER

"It sure would be nice to have a mother that somebody liked."
TERMS OF ENDEARMENT

"My mother—a waitress!"
MILDRED PIERCE

"I'm waiting tables at Jerry's Deli."
"I know the place—home of the famous cement Danish."
COCKTAIL

"Tell me, has there been a death in your family? This is funny stuff."
ARTHUR

"He told me he was a gynecologist. He couldn't speak any foreign languages. Who was he kidding?"
TAKE THE MONEY AND RUN

"It's not your being such a bastard that I object to—it's your being such a stupid bastard."
THE BEST MAN

"You almost scared me to death."
"Almost doesn't count."

WHERE'S POPPA?

"Why don't you mind your own business like
everybody else in New York?"

CACTUS FLOWER

"You're a very rude young woman . . ."
"I don't think I was treating her badly."
"Then you must be from New York."

TERMS OF ENDEARMENT

"I grant you [New York] is an exciting, vibrant,
stimulating, fabulous city, but it's not Mecca. It just
smells like it."

CALIFORNIA SUITE

"Everybody in the Bronx is ugly."

GUNS IN THE TREES

"Careful there! These [paintings] are worth more than
you'll ever make in a lifetime."

TERMS OF ENDEARMENT

"Gorgeous color, the smog. I wonder if they sell it in
bottles. It would make lovely gifts for back home."

CALIFORNIA SUITE

"One of the nicest qualities about you is that you
recognized your weaknesses. Don't lose the quality now
when you need it most."

TERMS OF ENDEARMENT

"You despise me, don't you?"
"If I gave you any thought, I probably would."

CASABLANCA

"Did anyone ever tell you that you have a dishonest
face—for a priest, I mean?"

THE BELLS OF ST. MARY'S

"Your tan is perfect. I always wondered how you get the back of your ears so dark."

CALIFORNIA SUITE

"Now that we're through with Humiliate the Host . . . and we don't want to play Hump the Hostess yet . . . how about a little round of Get the Guests?"

WHO'S AFRAID OF VIRGINIA WOOLF?

"Oh, I think it's a dream on you . . . It gives you a chin."

MIDNIGHT
complimenting woman on her hat

"Go and never darken my towels again."

DUCK SOUP

"Insanity runs in my family. It practically gallops."

ARSENIC AND OLD LACE

"You miserable, cowardly, wretched little caterpillar! Don't you ever want to become a butterfly?"

THE PRODUCERS

"You come to my office today like George God. Everybody's supposed to come up and audition for human being in front of you."

A THOUSAND CLOWNS

"Yes, you squashed cabbage leaf, you disgrace to the noble architecture of these columns . . . I can pass you off as the Queen of Sheba."

PYGMALION

"There are too many notes."

AMADEUS

"Vera, my old, old, *old* friend."

MAME

"You know what you are? You're a seventy-three-year-old schmo."

THE SUNSHINE BOYS

"My ancestors came over on the Mayflower."
"You're lucky. Now they have immigration laws."

THE HEAT'S ON

"May I ask you a personal question: Do you smile all the time?"

THE WAY WE WERE

"I wanna be just like you . . . all I need is a lobotomy and some tights."

THE BREAKFAST CLUB

"If you ever come to New York, try and find me."

THE MAN WHO CAME TO DINNER

"To those of you who do not read, attend the theater, or know anything of the world in which you live—it is perhaps necessary to introduce myself."

ALL ABOUT EVE

"Mr. Wilkes . . . can't be merely mentally faithful to his wife and won't be unfaithful to her technically."

GONE WITH THE WIND

"That's the wife of the Austrian critic. She always looks like she's been out in the rain feeding the poultry."

THE DARK CORNER

"Sure we're speaking, Jedediah. You're fired."

CITIZEN KANE

"You, a descendant of generations of inbred incestuous mental defectives—how dare you call anyone a barbarian."

CLEOPATRA

"You're the most beautiful woman I've ever seen, which doesn't say much for you."

ANIMAL CRACKERS

"If you'll be kind enough to glance between my shoulder blades . . . you'll find a knife buried to the hilt. On its handle are your initials."

A STAR IS BORN

"You're worse than a hopeless romantic. You're a hopeful one."

CALIFORNIA SUITE

"You're television incarnate, Diana, indifferent to suffering, insensitive to joy. All of life is reduced to the common rubble of banality. War, murder, death are all the same to you as bottles of beer."

NETWORK

"I wouldn't go on living with you if you were dipped in platinum."

THE AWFUL TRUTH

"I don't know how fast he moves. But it takes an early bird to get the best of a worm like me."

PILLOW TALK

"Go in and read the life of Florence Nightingale and learn how unfitted you are for your chosen profession."

THE MAN WHO CAME TO DINNER

"You must watch yourself, Mr. Kane. I'm telling you this for your own benefit. But you have the makings of an outstanding bore."

SABOTEUR

"Don't ever again, so long as you live, dare to call me uncle. By no stretch of the imagination could I possibly be a relative of yours."

SITTING PRETTY

"Elaine communicates with my brother and myself almost entirely by rumor."

A THOUSAND CLOWNS

"He was so crooked that when he died they had to screw him into the ground."

THE CAT AND THE CANARY

"I'm a man of one word: scram."

DUCK SOUP

"It should take you exactly four seconds to get from here to that door. I'll give you two."

BREAKFAST AT TIFFANY'S

"And now will you all leave quietly, or must I ask Miss Cutler to pass among you with a baseball bat."

THE MAN WHO CAME TO DINNER

"Eight days ago you showed up half-stoned for a simple nephrectomy, botched it, put the patient in failure and damn near killed him. Then—pausing only to send in your bill—you flew off . . ."

THE HOSPITAL

"Dr. Bradley is the greatest living argument for mercy killings."

THE MAN WHO CAME TO DINNER

"Don't look back or you'll turn into a pillar of salt and he'll sell you—eight dollars a pound."

ANOTHER PART OF THE FOREST

"You pay your way through life as though every relationship was a tollbooth."

SUMMER WISHES, WINTER DREAMS

"It's not a pretty face, I grant you, but underneath its flabby exterior is an enormous lack of character."

AN AMERICAN IN PARIS

"I don't like his face or any part of him. He looks like a Bulgarian bald eagle mourning its firstborn."

42ND STREET

"Don't point that finger at me unless you intend to use it."

THE ODD COUPLE

"Give thanks to God, Brighton, that when he made you a fool he gave you a fool's face."

LAWRENCE OF ARABIA

"Early nothing."

THE BIG HEAT
appraising living quarters

"If I kept my hair 'natural' the way you do, I'd be bald."

AUNTIE MAME

"You oughta put handles on that skull. Maybe you could grow geraniums in it."

THE LADY EVE

"He'll do or say anything to be loved by all. People like Frank ought to have two votes. Then they could mark their ballots Democrat and Republican . . ."

THE COUNTRY GIRL

"Your husband has a great deal to be modest about."

SITTING PRETTY

"This aging debutante I retain in my employ only because she is the sole support of her two-headed brother."

THE MAN WHO CAME TO DINNER

"You're a joke—a dirty joke, from one end of this town to the other."

BUTTERFIELD 8

"You were probably frightened by a callus at an early age."

MILDRED PIERCE

"Are you eating a tomato or is that your nose?"

YOU CAN'T CHEAT AN HONEST MAN

"I've never been able to understand why, when there's so much space in the world, people would deliberately choose to live in the middle west."

THE RAZOR'S EDGE

"I've met some hard-boiled eggs, but you—you're twenty minutes."

ACE IN THE HOLE

"I don't wanna break up the meeting or nothing, but she's something of a cunt, isn't she?"

ONE FLEW OVER THE CUCKOO'S NEST

"If you don't mind my mentioning it, Father, I think you have a mind like a swamp."

THE MIRACLE OF MORGAN'S CREEK

"It would be a terrific innovation if you could get your mind to stretch a little further than the next wisecrack."

STAGE DOOR

"Who writes your material for you? Charles Dickens?"

A THOUSAND CLOWNS

"You never pushed a noun against a verb except to blow up something."

INHERIT THE WIND

"I'll tell you what I think of newspapermen: The hand of God reaching down into the mire couldn't elevate one of them to the depths of degradation . . ."

NOTHING SACRED

"If you nurse as good as your sense of humor, I won't make it to Thursday."

THE SUNSHINE BOYS

"You call this a party? The beer is warm [and] the women are cold . . ."

MONKEY BUSINESS

"I wouldn't have you on a Christmas tree."

SERGEANT YORK

"I wouldn't have you if you were hung with diamonds, upside down."

FEMALE ON THE BEACH

"I may be rancid butter but I'm on your side of the bread."

INHERIT THE WIND

"I'm a bagel on a plate of onion rolls."

FUNNY GIRL

"I'm loud and I'm vulgar and I wear the pants in the house because somebody's got to, but I am not a monster."

WHO'S AFRAID OF VIRGINIA WOOLF?

"This may be the last chance I'll ever have to tell you to do anything, so I'm telling you: shut up."

GUESS WHO'S COMING TO DINNER

"Don't say 'stinks,' darling. If absolutely necessary, 'smells'—but only if absolutely necessary."

THE PHILADELPHIA STORY

"Frankly, you're beginning to smell—and for a stud in New York, that's a handicap."

MIDNIGHT COWBOY

"Do you know what I think, young fella? I think you're a newspaperman, I can smell 'em. I've always been able to smell 'em. Excuse me while I open a window."

NOTHING SACRED

"He's got a lot of charm."
"He comes by it naturally. His grandfather was a snake."

HIS GIRL FRIDAY

"Well, don't stand there, Miss Preen. You look like a frozen custard."

THE MAN WHO CAME TO DINNER

"George is bogged down in the History Department. He's an old bog in the History Department. That's what George is. A bog."

WHO'S AFRAID OF VIRGINIA WOOLF?

"I think you're a very stupid person. You look stupid.
You're in a stupid business. And you're on a stupid
case."
"I get it: I'm stupid."

FAREWELL, MY LOVELY

"You English, you're so fucking superior, aren't you?
Well, would you like to know where you'd be without
us to protect you? I'll tell you—the smallest fucking
province in the Russian empire . . ."

A FISH CALLED WANDA

"My whole life I have to suffer insults from this non-
person. This haircut that passes for a man."

HANNAH AND HER SISTERS

"I wouldn't believe anything you said if you had it
tattooed on your forehead."

GENTLEMEN PREFER BLONDES

"That is a *B*, darling—the first letter of a seven-letter
word that means your late father."

AUNTIE MAME

"I'm just a fat little man. A fat ugly man . . ."

MARTY

"He's the only man I know who can strut sitting
down."

INHERIT THE WIND

"Mister, the stork that brought you must have been a
vulture."

TORRID ZONE

"Kittredge is no great tower of strength . . . he's just a
tower."

THE PHILADELPHIA STORY

"Why don't you bore a hole in yourself and let the sap
run out?"

HORSE FEATHERS

"I would not like to get on the wrong side of him."
"Yes. He spits when he talks. . . ."

MURDER BY DEATH

"He's a natural phenomenon."
"So's acid rain."

CRIMES AND MISDEMEANORS

"I've underestimated you. You've started using your incompetence as a weapon."

BODY HEAT

"I wouldn't care to scratch your surface, because I know exactly what I'd find: instead of a heart, a handbag; instead of a soul, a suitcase; and instead of an intellect, a cigarette lighter which doesn't work."

THE SHOP AROUND THE CORNER

"My great-aunt Jennifer ate a whole box of candy every day of her life. She lived to be one hundred and two, and when she had been dead three days, she looked better than you do now."

THE MAN WHO CAME TO DINNER

"Haven't you heard of science's newest triumph—the doorbell?"

LAURA

"You're just not couth."

BORN YESTERDAY

CHAPTER
FIVE

★

Crime and
Cops

When you reflect on the great writers of crime films you think of Robert Benton and David Newman who wrote "Bonnie and Clyde," Dashiell Hammett, whose words in the novel *The Maltese Falcon* were so unforgettable; Agatha Christie whose mystery novels like *Murder on the Orient Express, And Then There Were None*, and short stories like "Witness for the Prosecution" kept audiences perennially perplexed. You recall Raymond Chandler who wrote the screenplay for Hitchcock's "Strangers on a Train" and whose Philip Marlowe novels formed the basis for "Murder, My Sweet" and "The Big Sleep"; and Ross Macdonald whose detective Lew Archer starred in films like "Harper" and "The Drowning Pool." Rarely does the colorful prose of detective-story writers manage to reach the screen. Hammett was most fortunate when John Huston adapted "The Maltese Falcon." Huston didn't try to improve on perfection, but simply had his secretary retype the novel in screenplay form. Of course, it is not easy to put memorable, cogent words in the mouths of cops and robbers, except perhaps for Dirty Harry who has a flair for economy (for example, "Read my lips," "Make my day," and so on). A Dashiell Hammett, who is able to write lines with color and punch for gangsters and private eyes, is rare. The most memorable words in "Dick Tracy" were Stephen Sondheim's lyrics, and the most provocative words in Pacino's "Scarface" were the copulative verbs. But in recent years there have been some Hollywood screenwriters who are nearly as eloquent with crime in film as Elmore Leonard is in print: the fascinating Coen Brothers in "Raising Arizona," David Ward in "The Sting," and Francis Coppola and Mario Puzo in their "Godfather" trilogy.

"Crisscross. I kill your victim, you kill mine."
STRANGERS ON A TRAIN

"He'll feel a lot better once we robbed a couple banks."
BUTCH CASSIDY AND THE SUNDANCE KID

"Forget it, Jake, it's Chinatown."
CHINATOWN

"The son-of-a-bitch stole my watch!"
THE FRONT PAGE

"We're going to steal the fabulous baseball diamond."
THE GREAT MUPPET CAPER

"Oh, there is a difference. The mob is run by murdering, cheating, thieving psychopaths. We work for the president of the United States."
MARRIED TO THE MOB

"Please put fifty thousand dollars into this bag. I am pointing a gun at you."
"That looks like 'gub' not 'gun.' "
TAKE THE MONEY AND RUN

"If I give up, the system gives up."
YEAR OF THE DRAGON

"What you doing wearing white man's clothes?"
IN THE HEAT OF THE NIGHT

"Prison is very structured—more than most people care for."

RAISING ARIZONA

"Will you send a patrol car? We have a burglar here. Just a moment, I'll see . . . Are you armed?"

THE GRADUATE

"There's no such thing as a bad boy."

BOYS TOWN

"Everything we wear, everything we eat, fell off a truck."

MARRIED TO THE MOB

"Criminals *want* to be caught. Eighteen of the twenty suspects arrested are known to have organized crime ties. If they don't want to get caught, don't wear the ties."

THINGS CHANGE

"Sometimes nothing is a very cool hand."

COOL HAND LUKE

"You need people like me so you can point your fucking fingers and say, 'That's the bad guy.' "

SCARFACE

"It's been almost a year since you've escaped."
"I haven't escaped—they're still after me. They'll always be after me."

I AM A FUGITIVE FROM A CHAIN GANG

"I didn't have the strength to resist corruption but I was strong enough to fight for a piece of it."

FORCE OF EVIL

"Michael, we're bigger than U.S. Steel!"

GODFATHER II

"Everything's just a little askew. Pretty soon people start thinking the old rules are no longer in effect."

BODY HEAT

"Never touch anyone on the street. They'll think you need help and they'll kill you."

CONTINENTAL DIVIDE

"Her womb is polluted."

SCARFACE

"I need a cake with a gun in it. And I need a dozen chocolate chip cookies with a bullet in each."

TAKE THE MONEY AND RUN

"Unfortunately, there is one thing that stands between me and that property, and that's the rightful owners."

BLAZING SADDLES

"I'd rather be thought of as a successful crook than a destitute monarch."

A KING IN NEW YORK

"Do not worry, Nathan Detroit's crap game will float again."

GUYS AND DOLLS

"He never made the ten-most-wanted list. It's very unfair voting. It's who you know."

TAKE THE MONEY AND RUN

"My daddy always said there's only one time a man should be in a hurry and that's when the cops are coming up the stairs."

GUYS AND DOLLS

"He's not as tough as he thinks."
"Neither are we."

THE STING

"He was wanted by federal authorities for dancing with a mailman."

TAKE THE MONEY AND RUN

"Do you take sinners here?"

GUYS AND DOLLS

"Fredo, you're my older brother and I love you, but don't ever take sides with anyone against the family . . . ever."

THE GODFATHER

"Nobody wears a beige suit to a bank robbery."

TAKE THE MONEY AND RUN

"One time he was sick and he wouldn't take penicillin because be bet his fever would go to one hundred and four."

GUYS AND DOLLS

"Can you get a mob together?"
"After what happened to Luther I don't think I can get more than two or three hundred guys."

THE STING

"So you're a private detective. I didn't know they existed, except in books—or else they were greasy little men snooping around hotel corridors."

THE BIG SLEEP

"I don't want my brother coming out of that toilet with just his dick in his hand."

THE GODFATHER

"One Rocco more or less isn't worth dying for."

KEY LARGO

"I'm sorry, Pepe. He thought you were going to escape."
"And so I am, my friend."

ALGIERS
*dying words from fatally
wounded criminal*

"It's not personal, Sonny, it's strictly business."

THE GODFATHER

"I think in order to be afraid, you got to have a heart. I don't think I got one. I had that cut out of me a long time ago."

ANGELS WITH DIRTY FACES

"Luca Brazzi held a gun to his head and my father assured him that either his brains or his signature would be on the contract."

THE GODFATHER

"He used to be a big shot."

THE ROARING TWENTIES

"Made it, Ma. Top of the world!"

WHITE HEAT

"I know what you're thinking. Did he fire six shots or only five. . . . You've got to ask yourself one question: Do I feel lucky?"

DIRTY HARRY

"What we've got here is a failure to communicate."

COOL HAND LUKE

"We didn't exactly believe your story. . . . We believed your two hundred dollars. . . . You paid us more than if you'd been telling us the truth and enough more to make it all right."

THE MALTESE FALCON

"How do you live?"
"I steal."

I AM A FUGITIVE FROM A CHAIN GANG

"Where does it say that you can't kill a cop?"

THE GODFATHER

"I suggest we give him ten years in Leavenworth or eleven years in Tensworth."

DUCK SOUP

"Office memorandum, 'Walter Neff to Barton Keyes, Claims Manager . . . Dear Keyes: I suppose you'll call this a confession . . .' "

DOUBLE INDEMNITY

"Kiss me, pig. . . . When I'm being fucked, I like to be kissed a lot."

DOG DAY AFTERNOON

"Mr. Norman Maine was apprehended driving an ambulance down Wilshire Boulevard—with the siren going full blast. He explained that he was a tree surgeon on a maternity case."

A STAR IS BORN

"We find the defendants incredibly guilty."

THE PRODUCERS

"That's not a knife . . . *that's* a knife."

CROCODILE DUNDEE

"I'm being marked down? I've been kidnapped by K-Mart."

RUTHLESS PEOPLE

"All right, let's play twenty questions. If you answer them correctly, maybe I won't knock your teeth out."

THE DARK CORNER

"A hand I could have sat in took hold of my shoulder."

FAREWELL, MY LOVELY

"The chances are you'll get off with life. That means if you're a good girl, you'll be out in twenty years. I'll be waiting for you."

THE MALTESE FALCON

"Everything is perfect—except for a couple of details."
"They hang people for a couple of details."

HAIL THE CONQUERING HERO

"There's a lot to be said for prison. You always know where you are when you get up in the morning."

WE'RE NO ANGELS

"Now just behave yourself, you two, and nobody'll get hurt. This is Duke Mantee, the world-famous killer. . . ."

THE PETRIFIED FOREST

"Killing a man with a sap's quiet, but it's no work for a lady."

MURDER, MY SWEET

"You know what I do with squealers? I let 'em have it in the belly so they can roll around for a long time thinking it over."

KISS OF DEATH

"Crime is a left-handed form of human endeavor."

THE ASPHALT JUNGLE

"You gentlemen aren't really trying to murder my son, are you?"

NORTH BY NORTHWEST

"He passed away two weeks ago and he bought the land a week ago . . . that's unusual."

CHINATOWN

"Wake up, it's time to die."

BLADE RUNNER

"Tell Victor that Ramon . . . went to the clinic today and I found out that I had Herpy Simplex Ten, and I think Victor should go check himself out . . . before things start falling off the man."

BEVERLY HILLS COP

"If you shoot me you'll lose a lot of these humanitarian awards."

FLETCH

"There's no overlooking the fact that murder is at our doorstep, so I wish you wouldn't drag it into the living room."

STRANGERS ON A TRAIN

". . . He was picked up in El Paso, Texas, for trying to smuggle a truckload of rich white Americans across the border into Mexico to pick melons."

MURDER BY DEATH

"What do you want?"
"My face on the one dollar bill."

BATMAN

"I don't like violence, Tom. I'm a businessman. Murder's a big expense."

THE GODFATHER

"When Saint Patrick drove the snakes out of Ireland, they swam to New York and joined the police force."

THE ICEMAN COMETH

"I caught the blackjack right behind the ear. A black pool opened up at my feet. I dived in. It had no bottom."

MURDER, MY SWEET

"Well, Wilmer, I'm sorry indeed to lose you . . . I couldn't be fonder of you if you were my own son. Well, if you lose a son, it's possible to get another. There's only one Maltese Falcon."

THE MALTESE FALCON

"I've never caught a jewel thief before. It's stimulating."

TO CATCH A THIEF

"Can somebody tell me what kind of a world we can live in where a man dressed as a bat gets all my press?"

BATMAN

"I love robbing the English, they're so polite."

A FISH CALLED WANDA

"What are you hanging your head for? What do you got to be ashamed of? You wanted to be a burglar so be a good one."

DETECTIVE STORY

"Nobody calls me a thief but the man I steals from."

MUTINY ON THE BOUNTY

"I did Shakespeare In The Park. . . . I got mugged. I was playing 'Richard III' and two guys with leather jackets stole my leotards."

ANNIE HALL

"I caught this guy stealing our water. Next time you try that, I'll let it out of you through little round holes."

THE TREASURE OF THE SIERRA MADRE

"That's a Sicilian message. It means 'Luca Brazzi sleeps with the fishes.' "

THE GODFATHER

"Okay, Marlowe . . . you're a tough guy. You've been sapped twice, choked, beaten silly with a gun, shot in the arm until you're as crazy as a couple of waltzing mice. Now, let's see you do something really tough—like putting on your pants."

MURDER, MY SWEET

"Suddenly, all the pieces fit together. I knew how the crime had been done. The high note on the trumpet that had shattered the glass."

THE BAND WAGON

"He was arrested in 1932 in Chicago for selling pornographic Bibles. . . . The D.A. couldn't make the charge stick when the church refused to turn over the Bibles."

MURDER BY DEATH

"If only I could steal enough to become an honest man."

AFTER THE FOX

"You have a bullet hole in your back."
"You should see the other guy."

MURDER BY DEATH

"Jail is no place for a young fellow. There's no advancement."

THE COCOANUTS

"People don't commit murder on credit."

DIAL M FOR MURDER

"You forgot—in your imbecilic devotion to your patient—that the punishment for two murders is the same as for one."

SPELLBOUND

"Philip Marlowe—name for a duke. You're just a nice mug."

MURDER, MY SWEET

"I always thought it was a ridiculous name for a prison—Sing Sing . . . Sounds like it should be an opera house. . . ."

BREAKFAST AT TIFFANY'S

"Murder victims have no claim to privacy."

LAURA

"Badges? We ain't got no badges. We don't need no badges. I don't have to show you any stinking badges."

THE TREASURE OF THE SIERRA MADRE

CHAPTER SIX

★

In a Word

"Rosebud."

CITIZEN KANE

"Stella!"

A STREETCAR NAMED DESIRE

"Sharks!"

JAWS

"La-dee-da."

ANNIE HALL

"Et cetera, et cetera, et cetera."

THE KING AND I

"Yowsah, yowsah, yowsah."

THEY SHOOT HORSES, DON'T THEY?

"Enter!"

THE SUNSHINE BOYS

"Tovarich! Tovarich!"

ACTION IN THE NORTH ATLANTIC

"Gosh!"

MY DINNER WITH ANDRÉ

"Water . . ."

THE MIRACLE WORKER

"Gin."

BORN YESTERDAY

"Plastics."

THE GRADUATE

CHAPTER
SEVEN

★

Politics

I t is the conventional wisdom in Hollywood that movies about politics don't do very well, and this has been borne out by results at the box office. Still, given the Hollywood-Washington connection and the fact that screenwriters are all political junkies, movies about politics keep turning up. Like Dr. Johnson said of second marriages, they are the conquest of hope over experience. It is a good thing that political movies do get made. Otherwise we would not have Gore Vidal's wonderfully witty dialogue in "The Best Man," and Allen Drury's sizzling novel "Advise and Consent" would never have been made into a Potomac soap opera by Otto Preminger; Lindsay and Crouse's wisecracks in their Broadway play *State of the Nation* would never have reached the screen on the lips of Tracy and Hepburn. And, of course, Jimmy Stewart would never have croaked his pleas to an indifferent Senate in "Mr. Smith Goes to Washington." (Interestingly, the U.S. Senate was so irate at Capra's inferences about venal congressmen that it promptly passed an Anti-Block-Booking Bill which cost Hollywood dearly.) There were many wonderful lines about politics in movies like "Casablanca," "Lawrence of Arabia," and "The Godfather," but for pure political dialogue nothing surpasses the rapier lines of Gore Vidal in "The Best Man." A page of his screenplay looks like a tray of jewelry.

"The women are behind Bill Russell."
"Under him is their more usual position."
THE BEST MAN

"If it wasn't for graft you'd get a very low type of people in politics."
HAIL THE CONQUERING HERO

"You all think I'm licked. Well, I'm not licked."
MR. SMITH GOES TO WASHINGTON

"Did you know that for every man in Washington D.C. there are four and a half women?"
MEDIUM COOL

"There was a time when you rich boys liked to play games like polo. Now you play politics."
THE BEST MAN

"If the senator has any complaints to make he ought to write a letter to his congressman."
ADVISE AND CONSENT

"I don't think a democratic system really works. Offer me a monarchy and we'll talk."
CALIFORNIA SUITE

"Politics has changed. When I was campaigning you had to pour your God over everything—like ketchup."
THE BEST MAN

"President's niece, huh! Say, before he's through, she'll be the president's wife."
CITIZEN KANE

"This is the bill that will convert the State Hospital for the Insane into the William J. Le Petomane Memorial Gambling Casino for the Insane."
BLAZING SADDLES

"Last week the Republicans paid a hundred dollars a plate for the very same food. Of course, it was fresh then."

THE CANDIDATE

"It's par for the course when you try to fool the people, but it's downright dangerous when you start to fool yourself."

ADVISE AND CONSENT

"My father's no different than any other powerful man . . . like a senator or a president. . . ."
"Senators and presidents don't have men killed."

THE GODFATHER

"If Don Corleone has all the judges and the politicians in New York then he must share them. . . . He must let us draw the water from the well."

THE GODFATHER

"Do your shy smile—the one the housewives adore."

THE BEST MAN

"When I came here, my eyes were big as question marks. Now they're big green dollar marks."

MR. SMITH GOES TO WASHINGTON

"Son, this is a Washington, D.C., kind of lie—that's where the other person knows you're lying and he knows you know."

ADVISE AND CONSENT

"When you think about it, the whole idea of two guys making decisions for twenty million people—that's pretty funny."

THE CANDIDATE

"I need, Don Corleone, those politicians that you carry in your pocket like so many nickels and dimes."

THE GODFATHER

"Being vice-president isn't exactly a crime—they can't put you in jail for it—but it is a sort of disgrace, like living in a mansion with no furniture."

ADVISE AND CONSENT

"We're all part of the same hypocrisy, Senator, but never think it applies to my family."

GODFATHER II

"There's nothing like a dirty low-down political fight to put the roses in your cheeks."

THE BEST MAN

"It's worse than horrible because a zombie has no will of his own. You see them sometimes walking about blindly, with dead eyes, following orders, not knowing what to do, not caring."
"You mean like Democrats."

THE GHOST BREAKERS

"You're the most beautiful plank in your husband's platform."

STATE OF THE UNION

"What do we do now?"

THE CANDIDATE
after winning election

"You'll excuse me, gentlemen. Your business is politics, mine is running a saloon."

CASABLANCA

"This is a man's world, Jeff, and you got to check your ideals outside the door like you do your rubbers."

MR. SMITH GOES TO WASHINGTON

"Why did God make so many dumb fools and Democrats?"

LIFE WITH FATHER

"Forty-two percent of all liberals are queer. That's a fact. The Wallace people took a poll."

JO

"Politics is a very peculiar thing. . . . If they want you, they want you. They don't need reasons anymore. They find their own reasons. It's just like when a girl wants a man."

HAIL THE CONQUERING HERO

"What have you been doing, standing over a hot resolution all day?"

BORN YESTERDAY

"There may be honor among thieves, but there's none in politicians."

LAWRENCE OF ARABIA

"We subsidize trains, we subsidize planes, why not subsidize people?"

THE CANDIDATE

"I wouldn't give you two cents for all your fancy rules if, behind them, they didn't have a little bit of plain, ordinary, everyday kindness. . . ."

MR. SMITH GOES TO WASHINGTON

"I paid for this microphone!"

STATE OF THE UNION

"Allie and I are united in the holy bonds of politics."

BEAU JAMES

"They're going to learn what democracy is if I have to shoot every one of them."

THE TEAHOUSE OF THE AUGUST MOON

"Don't tell me it's subversive to kiss a Republican."

A FOREIGN AFFAIR

"I don't think Matt would have made a great president, but I would have voted for him for king—just to have you for queen."

INHERIT THE WIND

"Politics? You couldn't get into politics. You couldn't get in anywhere. You couldn't get into the Men's Room at the Astor."

DINNER AT EIGHT

"Mr. President, I stand guilty as framed . . ."

MR. SMITH GOES TO WASHINGTON

"I apologize for the intelligence of my remarks. I had forgotten that you were a member of Parliament."

THE PICTURE OF DORIAN GRAY

"All that's bad around us is bad by selfishness. Sometimes, selfishness can even get to be a cause—an organized force, even a government. And then it's called fascism."

BORN YESTERDAY

"With Nixon in the White House, good health seemed to be in bad taste."

CALIFORNIA SUITE

"Our theater cannot compete with life in these melodramatic times. Politicians have stolen our tricks and blown them up into earth-sized, untidy productions and discarded the happy ending."

THE SAXON CHARM

"1954 was a pretty good year all around. It was the year we finally got rid of Joe McCarthy."

MY FAVORITE YEAR

"Petronius? Dead? By his own hand? I don't believe it. . . . Without my permission? It's rebellion!"

QUO VADIS

"Democracy is a system of self-determination. It's the right to make the wrong choice."

THE TEAHOUSE OF THE AUGUST MOON

CHAPTER
EIGHT

★

Show Business

Hollywood loves to make movies about Hollywood, Broadway, and Tin Pan Alley. The movies about pop culture come tumbling out of Hollywood like a thousand clowns pouring out of a circus Volkswagen. They come in every form: comedies, musicals, dramas, thrillers. The dialogue is usually crisp and cynical, in the tone that we usually ascribe to the people in show business. When screenwriters put words in the mouths of screenwriters, producers, or actors, they are generally brittle, bright, and cutting. Billy Wilder's dialogue in "Sunset Boulevard" is memorable. So are the words in various incarnations of "A Star Is Born." And the thirties musicals like "42nd Street," the "Gold Diggers" films, "Top Hat," and "Stage Door" are brisk and skeptical. Joe Mankiewicz's words about the theater in "All About Eve" are particularly quotable, as are Mel Brooks's in "The Producers." In recent years, Neil Simon's lines in "California Suite"—ascribed to actors and screenwriters—are funny and felicitous. And Norman Steinberg's script for "My Favorite Year" yields many witty lines set in the TV business of the fifties. Paddy Chayefsky, whose command of the language was formidable, drew the denizens of broadcasting in acid in his coruscating screenplay for "Network."

"Audiences don't know somebody sits down and writes a picture. They think the actors make it up as they go along."
SUNSET BOULEVARD

"And to think you can put those words down on paper like that and all I can do is hem brassieres."
SOME CAME RUNNING

"Let's put on a show!"
BABES IN ARMS

"It's show time!"
ALL THAT JAZZ

"Miss Caswell is an actress. A graduate of the Copacabana School of Dramatic Arts."
ALL ABOUT EVE

"Ah! There is something about Mozart."
"I think you're responding to his music."
LOVE AND DEATH

"You've got a 'lawyer acquaintance'? You must be an actor."
THE GOODBYE GIRL

"Gee, she looks better in person than on her album covers."
KING OF THE MOUNTAIN

"Don't tell me art. For thirty-two years in the [movie] industry I had every great writer working for me. Aldous Huxley, Robert Sherwood, Edgar Rice Burroughs."
WILL SUCCESS SPOIL ROCK HUNTER?

"Unfortunately, I learned to speak English correctly."
"That can't be much use to you here . . ."
STAGE DOOR

"I could always live in my art, but never in my life."

AUTUMN SONATA

"I'm going to make a comedy."

SULLIVAN'S TRAVELS

"I can't come in in the middle [of a movie]."
"The middle? We only missed the titles. They're in Swedish."

ANNIE HALL

"Three steps to the right, three steps to the left, and turn."

SWING TIME

Ginger showing Fred how to dance

"I wonder if future generations will even know about us."

RADIO DAYS

"Mulholland Drive is the first place where people talked about me when I wasn't there."

KING OF THE MOUNTAIN

"Are you appearing anywhere now?"
"Sure. You can catch me every Friday, at eleven o'clock, at the State Unemployment Office."

CACTUS FLOWER

"She got suspicious [about my playing for the philharmonic]. She asked me about Mozart and I couldn't place the name."

TAKE THE MONEY AND RUN

"You've got to have a sentimental reason for them to vote for you [for an Oscar]. Any decent actress can give a good performance but a dying husband would have insured everything."

CALIFORNIA SUITE

"The screens aren't bigger, the stars are smaller."

SUNSET BOULEVARD

"The blues is nothin' but a man losin' a good woman and feelin' bad."

CROSSROADS

"I know at the office I'm gruff Anthony Powell, theatrical producer. That's a pose. Here I'm just a tired little boy with a dream."

STAGE DOOR

"Want to know what the theater is? A flea circus. Also opera. Also rodeos, carnivals . . . the theater's for everybody—so don't approve or disapprove."

ALL ABOUT EVE

"[Hollywood]—it's like paradise with a lobotomy."

CALIFORNIA SUITE

"I *am* big. It's the *pictures* that got small."

SUNSET BOULEVARD

"What he did to Shakespeare, we are doing now to Poland."

TO BE OR NOT TO BE

"As an actor, no one could touch him. As a human being, no one wanted to touch him."

THE SUNSHINE BOYS

"If we bring a little joy into your humdrum lives, it makes us feel our work ain't been in vain for nothin'."

SINGIN' IN THE RAIN

"Don't big empty houses scare you?"
"Not me. I used to be in vaudeville."

THE CAT AND THE CANARY

"Have you lost your mind? How can you 'kill the actors'? . . . Actors are not animals. They're human beings."
"They are? Have you ever eaten with one?"

THE PRODUCERS

"I could cut your throat."

"If you did, greasepaint would run out of it."

TWENTIETH CENTURY

"A career is a curious thing. Talent isn't always enough. You need a sense of timing—an eye for seeing the turning point. . . ."

A STAR IS BORN

"Being an actor's wife is not the easiest of jobs. If I tell him he's magnificent, he says I'm not being honest—if I tell him he's not magnificent, he says I don't love him."

THE COUNTRY GIRL

"A week? Are you kidding? This play has got to close on page four."

THE PRODUCERS

"Every goddamn executive fired from a network in the last twenty years has written this dumb book about the early years of television. And nobody wants the dumb, damn, goddamn book about the early years of television."

NETWORK

"It's bizarre. Eight years with the National Theatre, two Pinter plays, nine Shakespeare, three Shaw—and I finally get nominated for a nauseating little comedy."

"That's why they call it Hollywood."

CALIFORNIA SUITE

"I hate that word [comeback]. It's *return*—a return to the millions of people who've never forgiven me for deserting the screen."

SUNSET BOULEVARD

"I danced in my mother's womb."

ISADORA

"He's perhaps the worst director that ever lived. He's the only director whose plays close on the first day of rehearsal."

THE PRODUCERS

"Television is not the truth. Television is a goddamn amusement park . . . we're in the boredom-killing business."

NETWORK

"My wife was so twisted she once said to me, 'I hope your next play's a flop—so the whole world can see how much I love you, even though you're a failure.' "

THE COUNTRY GIRL

"You know, this floor used to be wood, but I had it changed. Valentino said there's nothing like tile for the tango."

SUNSET BOULEVARD

"Max Bialstock, King of Broadway! Six shows running at once. Lunch at Delmonico's! Two-hundred-dollar suits! Look at me now. I'm wearing a cardboard belt."

THE PRODUCERS

"This is Sweet Sue, saying good night, reminding all you daddies out there that every girl in my band is a virtuoso, and I intend to keep it that way."

SOME LIKE IT HOT

"He was a king in the world he knew, but now he comes to civilization merely a captive—a show to gratify your curiosity. Ladies and gentlemen, look at Kong."

KING KONG

"You know what your trouble was, Willie? You always took the jokes too seriously. They were just jokes. We did comedy on the stage for forty-three years. I don't think you enjoyed it once."

THE SUNSHINE BOYS

"Go out there and be so swell you'll make me hate you."

42ND STREET

"I've got to have more steps. I need more steps. I've got to get higher . . . higher . . ."

THE GREAT ZIEGFELD

"You can't hurt me. I always wear a bulletproof vest around the studio."

HELLZAPOPPIN

"This is Sunset Boulevard, Los Angeles, California. It's about five o'clock in the morning . . . a murder has been reported from one of those great big houses in the ten thousand block. . . ."

SUNSET BOULEVARD

"The most beautiful poems about England in the spring were written by poets living in Italy at the time."

THE GHOST AND MRS. MUIR

"A sculptor friend of [mine] used this room for about six months . . . such talented fingers, but oh, what he did to my bust."

AUNTIE MAME

"To be on the wire is alive—the rest is waiting."

ALL THAT JAZZ

"I'm a movie star—I'm not an actor!"

MY FAVORITE YEAR

"Move a few decimal points around. You can do it. You're an accountant. You're in a noble profession."

THE PRODUCERS

"Those movies you were in! Sacrilege . . . when I left that movie house, I felt some magnificent ruby had been thrown into a platter of lard."

TWENTIETH CENTURY

"I've had it! . . . 'The Girl From the Sleepy Lagoon,' 'The Cowboy and the Mermaid,' 'Neptune's Mother.' I never get a chance to dry off. From now on I am just going to swim socially.''

SILK STOCKINGS

''Ed hates everything that keeps him from going to the movies every night. I guess I'm what you call a Garbo widow.''

DINNER AT EIGHT

''What would you fellas say to an assassination? I think I can get the Mao Tse-tung people to kill Beale for us as one of the shows. In fact, it'd make a helluva kickoff show for the season.''

NETWORK

''Music is essential for parades.''

SILK STOCKINGS

''If you can't paint in Paris, you'd better give up and marry the boss's daughter.''

AN AMERICAN IN PARIS

''I left home at the age of four, and I haven't been back since. They can hear me on the radio, and that's enough for them.''

THE MAN WHO CAME TO DINNER

''Whenever you put about fifty artists together in a room you get a really pleasant combination of gossip, paranoia, envy, fear, trembling, hatred, lust, and pretense.''

AN UNMARRIED WOMAN

''It's about time the piano realized it has not written the concerto.''

ALL ABOUT EVE

''The enjoyment of art is the only remaining ecstasy that's neither immoral nor illegal.''

THE DARK CORNER

"We [agents] have those offices high up there so that we can catch the wind and go with it, however it blows."

A THOUSAND CLOWNS

"A dozen press agents working overtime can do terrible things to the human spirit."

SUNSET BOULEVARD

"You don't know what it means to know that . . . a whole audience just doesn't want you."

CITIZEN KANE

"How could this happen? I was so careful. I picked the wrong play. The wrong director, the wrong cast—where did I go right?"

THE PRODUCERS

"He wants to talk to you about [making] a neo-realistic picture."
"What's neo-realism?"
"No money."

AFTER THE FOX

"You don't have to tell me about the immaturity of actors. I was raised by two."

HANNAH AND HER SISTERS

"That's not acting. That's kissing and jumping and drinking and humping."

MY FAVORITE YEAR

"You think you can play the lead tonight?"
"The lead?"

42ND STREET

"The last [movie script] I wrote was about Okies in the dust bowl. You'd never know because, when it reached the screen, the whole thing played on a torpedo boat."

SUNSET BOULEVARD

"Kirk was wrong when he said I didn't know where movie scripts left off and life began. A script has to make sense, and life doesn't."

THE BAREFOOT CONTESSA

"It's been ages since I sat in front of the TV just changing channels . . . Nazis, deodorant salesmen, and wrestlers . . ."

HANNAH AND HER SISTERS

"That's all television is, my dear. Nothing but auditions."

ALL ABOUT EVE

"It's theater [and] I got it right in there up to my armpits."
"That's higher than usual."

THE BAND WAGON

"Sidney, I have just thrown up in front of the best people in Hollywood. Now is no time to be sensitive."

CALIFORNIA SUITE

"I'm a concert pianist. That's a pretentious way of saying I'm unemployed at the moment."

AN AMERICAN IN PARIS

"Do you know what I like about your program? Even when I'm running the vacuum, I can understand it."

A LETTER TO THREE WIVES

"My native habitat is the theater. In it I toil not, neither do I spin. I am a critic and commentator. I am essential to the theater—as ants to a picnic. . . ."

ALL ABOUT EVE

"This time, humor the writers. Say *some* of their lines."

MY FAVORITE YEAR

"You try leading the Charge of the Light Brigade wearing a corset, they'll laugh you right off the screen."

AFTER THE FOX

"Show business is dog eat dog. It's worse than dog eat dog. It's dog doesn't return other dog's phone calls."

CRIMES AND MISDEMEANORS

"What about Eddie Clark's Penguin? . . . The penguin skates on the stage dressed as a rabbi."

BROADWAY DANNY ROSE

"I was listening to the Beethoven Ninth. Somewhere on this plane there is a wonderful orchestra."

CALIFORNIA SUITE

"I'm not coming back till I know what trouble is."

SULLIVAN'S TRAVELS

"Bessie let her hair grow and is playing with Stokowski."

SOME LIKE IT HOT

"I taught you everything you know. Even your name, Lily Garland—I gave you that. If there is a justice in heaven, Mildred Plotka, you will end up where you belong . . ."

TWENTIETH CENTURY

"If there's nothing else there's applause . . . It's like waves of love coming over the footlights and wrapping you up. Imagine, to know every night that different hundreds of people love you."

ALL ABOUT EVE

"My mother thanks you, my father thanks you, my sister thanks you, and I thank you."

YANKEE DOODLE DANDY

CHAPTER NINE

★

Love and Romance

For half a century the movies have been concentrating on the period *before* couples get married. Screenwriters have focused on the "cute meet" and the romance that follows. Movie stories, in the words of George Kaufman, have three steps: "Boy meets girl, girl gets boy in pickle, boy gets pickle in girl." Once the couple is married, their story is less intriguing. Marriage is viewed as a dull meal with the dessert at the beginning. Thus, screenwriters often seem better equipped to write about love and romance than about love in marriage. In films like "Marty," "A Place in the Sun," "Now, Voyager," "Body Heat," "Annie Hall," "Picnic," "The Heiress," "What's Up, Doc?" "Carnal Knowledge," and "Ninotchka," the principals are unmarried and joust on a road that we know will end in marriage or regret or both. It might be expected that all these movie lines about love would be sweet enough to rot the teeth at twenty paces. They are not. Many have a tart or ironic taste to them; many are offensive and combative. One thing is certain: Screenwriters have the gift for bringing perennial freshness to the familiar subject of love, and that is no mean feat.

"Have you ever been in love?"

"No, I've been a bartender all my life."

THE OX-BOW INCIDENT

"To love is to suffer. Not to love is to suffer. To suffer is to suffer."

LOVE AND DEATH

"I love you. I've loved you from the first moment I saw you. I've loved you *before* I saw you."

A PLACE IN THE SUN

"I've grown accustomed to her face."

PYGMALION

"She wanted to break off the engagement and so he started cleaning guns in his mouth."

THE ODD COUPLE

"Anything you ask of me I'll do, except one thing: I won't watch you die. I'll miss that scene if you don't mind."

BUTCH CASSIDY AND THE SUNDANCE KID

"I like him."

"He's away most of the time."

"I like him even better."

BODY HEAT

"It's probably their first date . . . She met him by answering an ad in the *New York Review of Books.* Thirtyish academic wishes contact with woman who likes James Joyce, Mozart, and sodomy."

ANNIE HALL

"You go your way and I'll go my way."

HELLO, DOLLY!

"Take your key and open post-office box two thirty-seven and take me out of my envelope and kiss me."

THE SHOP AROUND THE CORNER

"If God gave me this woman, then there must be a God."

SALVADOR

"She's very nice. I like her very much. It means a lot to me and I want you to know if you mess this one up for me, I'm gonna punch your fucking heart out."

WHERE'S POPPA?

"Do you want to come in?"
"I'd rather stick needles in my eyes."

TERMS OF ENDEARMENT

"You played it for her and you can play it for me . . . if she can stand it, I can. Play it!"

CASABLANCA

"I knew I was in love. First of all, I was very nauseous."

TAKE THE MONEY AND RUN

"Don't worship me until I've earned it."

TERMS OF ENDEARMENT

"Never came poison from so sweet a place."

RICHARD III

"Oh, Your Excellency!"
"You're not bad yourself."

DUCK SOUP

"Shall we just have a cigarette on it?"

NOW, VOYAGER

"I'd love to kiss yuh, but I just washed my hair."

CABIN IN THE COTTON

"Would you hang us together, please?"

THE AFRICAN QUEEN

"Isn't it enough that you've gathered every other man's heart today? You've always had mine. You cut your teeth on it."

GONE WITH THE WIND

"Was that cannon fire, or is it my heart pounding?"

CASABLANCA

"Everything was his idea, except my leaving him."

CITIZEN KANE

"You don't know what love means. To you, it's just another four-letter word."

CAT ON A HOT TIN ROOF

"I don't know how to kiss or I would kiss you. Where do the noses go?"

FOR WHOM THE BELL TOLLS

"It must be a marvelous supper. We may not eat it but it must be marvelous. And, waiter, you see that moon? I want that moon in the champagne."

TROUBLE IN PARADISE

"When you brought the roses, I felt something stir in me that I thought was dead forever."

THE SUBJECT WAS ROSES

"If you take my heart by surprise, the rest of my body has the right to follow."

TOM JONES

"Mr. Kralik, it's true we're in the same room, but we're not in the same planet."
"Why Miss Novak . . . you certainly know how to put a man in his planet."

THE SHOP AROUND THE CORNER

"With a binding like you've got, people are going to want to know what's in the book."

AN AMERICAN IN PARIS

"The only difference between a caprice and a lifelong passion is that the caprice lasts a little longer."

THE PICTURE OF DORIAN GRAY

"I can't send you flowers, baby, but I can send you."

PICNIC

"Every time I get affectionate with you, I feel as if I'm snuggling up to the Taft-Hartley Bill."

JUNE BRIDE

"He has grown greedier with the years. The first time he wanted my money. This time he wants my love, too."

THE HEIRESS

"One false move and I'm yours."

THE COCOANUTS

"Love is like the measles. You only get it once. The older you are, the tougher it goes."

SEVEN BRIDES FOR SEVEN BROTHERS

"That was restful. Again."

NINOTCHKA
Garbo learning how to kiss

"Life is very long and full of salesmanship, Miss Clara. You might buy something yet."

THE LONG, HOT SUMMER

"Love is a miracle. It's like a birthmark. You can't hide it."

BLUME IN LOVE

"You have a passion for respectability and I have a horror of loneliness—that's love."

THE GODDESS

"My love for you is the only malady I've contracted since the usual childhood diseases, and it's incurable."

THE DARK CORNER

"Everybody on this ship is in love. Love me whether or not I love you. Love me whether I am fit to love. Love me whether I am able to love."

SHIP OF FOOLS

"You ever been in love, Hornbeck?"
"Only with the sound of my own words, thank God."

INHERIT THE WIND

"If you had the choice . . . would you rather love a girl or have her love you?"

CARNAL KNOWLEDGE

"Just say you love me. You don't have to mean it."

THE BACHELOR PARTY

"Your dream prince, reporting for duty."

ROSE MARIE

"Take me to the window. Let me look at the moors with you once."

WUTHERING HEIGHTS

"Moses, you stubborn, splendid, adorable fool."

THE TEN COMMANDMENTS

"You give me powders, pills, baths, injections, and enemas—when all I need is love."

THE BRIDGE ON THE RIVER KWAI

"Wilt thou love her?"
"From the bottom of my soul to the tip of my penis. . . ."

THE RULING CLASS

"Ya wanna dance or would you rather just suck face?"

ON GOLDEN POND

"The Venus' flytrap—a devouring organism, aptly named for the goddess of love."

SUDDENLY LAST SUMMER

"Your love affair with yourself has reached heroic proportions. It doesn't leave much room for me."

POSSESSED

"Please promise me never to wear black satin or pearls, or to be thirty-six years old."

REBECCA

"You know me, I'm like you. It's two in the morning and I don't know nobody."

THE STING

"I'm just a hack writer who drinks too much and falls in love with girls. You."

THE THIRD MAN

"I was bored to death. I hadn't seen one attractive woman on this ship since we left . . . and then I saw you and I was saved."

"Tell me, have you been getting results with a line like that . . . ?"

AN AFFAIR TO REMEMBER

"Go on, Heathcliff. Run away. Bring me back the world."

WUTHERING HEIGHTS

"He was one of our great scientists. He has proved, beyond any question, that physical attraction is purely electrochemical."

SILK STOCKINGS

"I used to make obscene phone calls to her collect— and she used to accept the charges."

TAKE THE MONEY AND RUN

"You don't have to act with me, Steve. You don't have to say anything. And you don't have to do anything. Not a thing. Oh, maybe just whistle. You know how to whistle, don't you, Steve? You just put your lips together and blow."

TO HAVE AND HAVE NOT

"In the spring a young man's fancy lightly turns to what he's been thinking about all winter."

MILDRED PIERCE

"Someone has killed herself for love of you. I do wish that I had had such an experience. The women who have admired me . . . have all insisted on living on long after I have ceased to care for them . . ."

THE PICTURE OF DORIAN GRAY

"It's midnight. Look at the clock. One hand has met the other hand. They kiss. Isn't that wonderful?"

NINOTCHKA

"Love flies out the door when money comes innuendo."

MONKEY BUSINESS

"You know how many good kissers are starving in Italy?"

AFTER THE FOX

CHAPTER
TEN

★

War and
the Military

Movie makers have generally approached war as though it were a narrative of heroic fiction. They seldom deal with the political, moral, humane, or even military issues of war. For decades the movies have sanitized and romanticized the Second World War almost beyond recognition. During the war itself, the military used the movies like press releases. There was a publicity competition among the services: The Marine Corps was first with "Wake Island," the Army retaliated with "Bataan," then came the Air Corps with "Air Force," then the Navy with "Destination Tokyo," and finally the merchant marine with "Lifeboat." The damage the war visited on bodies is obvious. Less obvious is the damage it did to intellect and honesty and wit. "Rambo" was not the first to turn the horror and suffering of war into a loony, bloodthirsty, patriotic computer game. It is the rare screenwriter who has approached the subject of war with honesty and wit: Francis Coppola in "Patton" and "Apocalypse Now," Oliver Stone in "Platoon," Robert Bolt in "Lawrence of Arabia," Daniel Taradash in James Jones's "From Here to Eternity," Buck Henry in Joseph Heller's

"Catch-22," and in the scalding performance of George C. Scott in "Dr. Strangelove."

"No bastard ever won a war by dying for his country."

PATTON

"You're talking about mass murder, General, not war."
"I'm not saying we wouldn't get our hair mussed."

DR. STRANGELOVE

"They were *all* disloyal. I tried to run the ship properly by the book, but they fought me at every turn."

THE CAINE MUTINY

"I love the smell of napalm in the morning."

APOCALYPSE NOW

"There was a fever over the land."

JUDGMENT AT NUREMBERG

"Catch-22—that's a terrific catch."

CATCH-22

"Is green the only color these come in?"

PRIVATE BENJAMIN

"From now on you clean the mess hall *and* the latrine!"
"How will I tell the difference?"

STRIPES

"Did you kill last week? Did you *try* to kill last week?"

HISTORY OF THE WORLD—PART I
to gladiator on unemployment line

"Are you homosexuals?"
"We're not, but we're willing to learn."

STRIPES
duo enlisting in the Army

"This is desertion in the face of the enemy!"
"I ain't got no more enemies."

THE SAND PEBBLES

"What are you thinking of, coming here dressed like that, amateur theatricals?"
"Yes."

LAWRENCE OF ARABIA

"Do you think the men will like this? It's chocolate cotton."

CATCH-22

"One murder makes a villain, millions a hero."

MONSIEUR VERDOUX

"As soon as my husband comes back, I'm going to be busy at home."

ROSIE THE RIVETER

"Take that man out and shoot him."

CATCH-22

"Now they're making jock straps out of the flag."

SAVE THE TIGER

"Throw the wog out!"

LAWRENCE OF ARABIA

"No, I'm not a major, my name is Captain Major."

CATCH-22

"Have you ever been convicted of a felony or a misdemeanor?"
"Convicted?"

STRIPES

"They don't want a revolution."
"Yes they do. They don't know it yet, but that's what they want."

DOCTOR ZHIVAGO

"Dropping a bomb is like telling a lie."

THE MISFITS

"I want to understand. I do want to understand. I have to."

JUDGMENT AT NUREMBERG

"You can't fight in here—this is the War Room."

DR. STRANGELOVE

"My mouth belongs where I put it."

REVOLUTION

"Hail, Fredonia . . ."

DUCK SOUP

"The horror . . ."

APOCALYPSE NOW

"How can one country offend another? You mean, there's a mountain over in Germany that gets mad at a field over in France?"

ALL QUIET ON THE WESTERN FRONT

"Those people in the French Resistance were brave. To have to listen to Maurice Chevalier so much."

ANNIE HALL

"Shoot, a fella could have a pretty good weekend in Vegas with all that stuff."

DR. STRANGELOVE
*finding his survival kit
contains money, a Bible,
condoms, and nylons*

"Are we going to do this again?"

JUDGMENT AT NUREMBERG

"It's the French, isn't it? It's usually the French."

OH! WHAT A LOVELY WAR
*asked who the British are
fighting in the Crimea*

"Most of 'em got nothing. They're poor, they're the unwanted . . . They're the best I've ever seen, Grandma . . ."

PLATOON

"Tell me, Robbie. What's wrong with her?"
"Props. Gear. One wing tip. That's all."

AIR FORCE

"Listen, any buck-toothed little runt can walk up behind Joe Louis and knock him cold with a baseball bat."

ACROSS THE PACIFIC

"Dear Wheeler—you provide the prose poems—I'll provide the war."

CITIZEN KANE

"Who are you?"
"Your worst nightmare."

RAMBO III

"Can't we just see the end?"
"They've got the real thing outside."
"It's not the same."

HOPE AND GLORY
*child watching war film
during the blitz*

"In years to come, this will be the greatest adventure we ever had, though we had it separately."

MRS. MINIVER

"The only thing that blows your mind when you're thirty is getting guys to kill other guys, only in another city, another country, where you don't see it."

WILD IN THE STREETS

"Today's lecture is on the friendly use of nuclear weapons."

SOLDIER GIRLS

"Have you ever been up in your plane, alone, at night, somewhere twenty thousand feet above the ocean . . . ? Did you ever hear music up there . . . ? It's the music man's spirit sings . . ."

A GUY NAMED JOE

"That's for Pearl Harbor, you slant-eyed . . ."

LITTLE TOKYO USA

"Feelings, insights, affections—they're all suddenly trivial now. The private life is dead for a man with any manhood."

DOCTOR ZHIVAGO

"A lot of people in this state still expect an invasion in Pasadena."

THE CANDIDATE

"We weren't fighting. We were fighting ourselves."

PLATOON

"It's not war—war's between soldiers. It's murder— murder of innocent people."

BLOCKADE

"If we'd had our twelve fighters up, we'd have smeared them. But we were listening on the shortwave to Tokyo telling about Mr. Kurusu's peace mission . . ."

ACROSS THE PACIFIC

"Unfortunately, in time of war, the loyal must suffer inconvenience with the disloyal. Be vigilant, America!"

LITTLE TOKYO USA

"Not what we are used to at the country club."

SINCE YOU WENT AWAY
genteel wife at welding job

"There's nothing especially Japanese about this. . . . You'll find it wherever you find fascists. There are even people who call themselves American who can do it, too."

OBJECTIVE BURMA

"Appeasement has come home to roost, men."

DESTINATION TOKYO

"He sure as hell won't let [the Russians] land on the beach at Santa Monica. The parking problem is bad enough already."

THE CANDIDATE

"How can you talk about musicals at a time like this? With the world committing suicide . . . corpses piling up in the street, people slaughtered like sheep."

SULLIVAN'S TRAVELS

"I'm a Vietnam Veteran. I fought in Vietnam and I gotta right to be treated decently."

BORN ON THE FOURTH OF JULY

"Do I get a vote too?"

LIFEBOAT
black man in lifeboat

"The [territory's] mine."
"By what authority?"
"It's got my troops all over it."

THE LION IN WINTER

"This is not a nice man."

WHICH WAY TO THE FRONT?
referring to Adolf Hitler

"To survive a war you have to become war."

RAMBO: FIRST BLOOD, PART II

"Please don't worry if our precious well-bred hands come in contact with their mangled bodies. We'll survive. Even if they don't."

SINCE YOU WENT AWAY

"We will tolerate no guerrillas in the casinos or the swimming pools."

GODFATHER II

"Hey Ron . . . hey peace, brother . . . I'm in the National Guard. I love my country."

BORN ON THE FOURTH OF JULY

"The lights have gone out in Europe! Hang on to your lights, America—they're the only lights still on in the world!"

FOREIGN CORRESPONDENT

"A Jap is a Jap."

ACROSS THE PACIFIC

"Exterminate him! Exterminate them all!"

LIFEBOAT

"Now that I'm going home, I'm scared. I wasn't half as scared on Guadalcanal as I am now."

PRIDE OF THE MARINES

"We live in the trenches out there. We fight. We try not to be killed. But sometimes we are. That's all."

ALL QUIET ON THE WESTERN FRONT

"Oh, but the strawberries. That's where I had them. They laughed and made jokes, but I proved beyond a shadow of a doubt, and with geometric logic, that a duplicate key to the wardroom icebox did exist."

THE CAINE MUTINY

"You got no right to call me a murderer. You have a right to kill me and you have the right to do that—but you have no right to judge me."

APOCALYPSE NOW

"I love the Army. A man loves a thing, that doesn't mean it's got to love him back."

FROM HERE TO ETERNITY

"Now, here's to the real author of 'The Caine Mutiny,' here's to you, Mr. Keefer."

THE CAINE MUTINY

"There are two things necessary to salvation. . . . Money and gunpowder."

MAJOR BARBARA

"So they call me Concentration Camp Ehrhardt."

TO BE OR NOT TO BE

"Ninotchka, let me confess something. Never did I dream I could feel this toward a sergeant."

NINOTCHKA

"Anyone who wants to get out of combat isn't really crazy, so I can't ground him."

CATCH-22

"Dreaming won't get you to Damascus, sir, but discipline will."

LAWRENCE OF ARABIA

"You Roman generals become divine so quickly."

CLEOPATRA

"Out here, due process is a bullet."

THE GREEN BERETS

"I'm thinking now of . . . all the guys everywhere who sail from tedium to apathy and back again with an occasional side trip to monotony."

MISTER ROBERTS

"The English have a great hunger for desolate places. I fear they hunger for Arabia."

LAWRENCE OF ARABIA

"Here's a soldier of the South who loves you, Scarlett, wants to feel your arms around him. . . . You're a woman sending a soldier to his death. . . . Scarlett, kiss me."

GONE WITH THE WIND

"The big brass are going to yell their heads off about this. And the Japanese aren't going to like it much either. Have you got anything to say to them, sir?"
"Yeah. Tell 'em we said *Sayonara*."

SAYONARA

"You may tell the crew for me there are four ways of doing things on board my ship: the right way, the wrong way, the Navy way, and my way. If they do things my way, we'll get along."

THE CAINE MUTINY

"I can no longer sit back and allow the international communist conspiracy to sap and impurify all our precious bodily fluids."

DR. STRANGELOVE

"We have ways of making men talk."

LIVES OF THE BENGAL LANCERS

"In Italy for thirty years under the Borgias, they had warfare, terror, murder, bloodshed. They produced Michelangelo, Leonardo da Vinci, and the Renaissance. In Switzerland they had brotherly love, five hundred years of democracy and peace, and what did they produce—the cuckoo clock."

THE THIRD MAN

"The Russians are coming! The Russians are coming! The Russians are coming!"

THE RUSSIANS ARE COMING THE
RUSSIANS ARE COMING

"Captain, it is I, Ensign Pulver, and I just threw your stinking palm tree overboard. Now what's all this crud about no movie tonight?"

MISTER ROBERTS

"For me there is no peace while you live, Mongol!"
"Say, yer beautiful in yer wrath."

THE CONQUEROR

"I'm adamant. I will not have an officer from my battalion working as a coolie."

THE BRIDGE ON THE RIVER KWAI

"Armies have marched over me."

FIRE DOWN BELOW

"He was a poet, a scholar, and a mighty warrior. . . . He was also the most shameless exhibitionist since Barnum and Bailey."

LAWRENCE OF ARABIA

"Sometimes I wonder whose side God's on."

THE LONGEST DAY

"Rommel, you beautiful bastard. I read your book."

PATTON

"One shot is what it's all about. The deer has to be taken with one shot."

THE DEER HUNTER

"Why are you nervous? This isn't have-a-gimp-over-for-dinner night, is it?"

COMING HOME

"Goddamn it, I'd piss on a spark plug if I thought it would do any good."

WARGAMES

"Go-o-od morning, Vietnam!"

GOOD MORNING, VIETNAM

"You write only about yourself. You think this whole war's a show put on for you to cover like a Broadway show. And if enough people die before the last act, maybe you might give it four stars."

LIFEBOAT

"In my country, General, they say, 'Never blow a bridge until you come to it.' "

FOR WHOM THE BELL TOLLS

"Most of the miseries of the world were caused by wars. And when they were over, no one knew what they were about."

GONE WITH THE WIND

"Some of us prefer Austrian voices raised in song to ugly German threats."

THE SOUND OF MUSIC

"That's exactly why we want to produce this play: to show the world the true Hitler—the Hitler you loved, the Hitler you knew, the Hitler with a song in his heart."

THE PRODUCERS

"If you think there is no science in a cat-o'-nine-tails, you should see my bos'n."

MUTINY ON THE BOUNTY

"An army is a team. It lives, eats, sleeps, fights as a team. This individuality stuff is a bunch of crap. The bilious bastards who write that stuff about individuality for the *Saturday Evening Post* don't know anything more about real battle than they do about fornication."

PATTON

"I've talked with the responsible leaders of the great powers—England, France, Germany, and Italy. They're too intelligent to embark on a project which would mean the end of civilization as we now know it. You can take my word for it: There'll be no war!"

CITIZEN KANE

"Fiddle-dee-dee. War, war, war. This war talk's spoiling all the fun at every party this spring."

GONE WITH THE WIND

"Well, boys, I guess this is it: nuclear combat, toe to toe, with the Russkies."

DR. STRANGELOVE

"You think you're sending me to my doom, eh? Well, you're wrong. . . . I'll live to see you hang from the highest yardarm in the British fleet."

MUTINY ON THE BOUNTY

"Kill every officer in sight."
"Ours or theirs?"

THE DIRTY DOZEN

"This picture takes place in Paris in those wonderful days when a siren was a brunette and not an alarm. . . ."

NINOTCHKA

"There is only one way to deal with Rome . . . you must serve her. You must abase yourself before her. You must grovel at her feet. You must love her."

SPARTACUS

"How can they give you a medal for a war they don't even want you to fight?"

COMING HOME

"Oh dear, Yankees in Georgia! How did they ever get in?"

GONE WITH THE WIND

"We make our tortillas out of corn, not patience—and patience will not cross an armed fence."

VIVA ZAPATA!

"It doesn't take much to see that the problems of three little people don't amount to a hill of beans in this crazy world."

CASABLANCA

"They're trying to kill me."

CATCH-22

"Goddamn army . . . goddamn army."

M*A*S*H

CHAPTER
ELEVEN

★

Wealth and Poverty

In the thirties, Hollywood applied humor to the wounds of the Depression. In the Capraesque Depression parables there was always a muted echo of the warfare between the rich and poor. There was also a cross-class learning experience, and the inevitable last-minute renunciation of snobbery. This was not an entirely faithful picture of the chasm between the people at the top and the bottom of the pyramid. The classic movie about rich and poor was "My Man Godfrey" and concerned the reforming of a wealthy and amoral New York family by a derelict. Hollywood acclimated us to these people in evening clothes who had white telephones. Movies also gave us a quick look at the other end of the spectrum in "The Grapes of Wrath," but the middle class preferred to look at the rich enjoying their riches rather than the poor suffering their poverty. "Meet John Doe" even suggested that the poor had a great deal of power, and Frank Capra's talent almost made us believe it. In "Annie," Tom Meehan replicated this painful era in sentimental strokes. Generally, Hollywood and its scribes concocted the comfortable fiction that the wealthy were fumbling and discontented. "Arthur" was a recent (and hilarious) film that pictured the futility of a wealthy existence and the endearing traits of the wealthy. The trick of making the powerful seem victimized and appealing was pulled off by Edna Ferber in "Giant," Bernard Shaw in "Major Barbara," and Tennessee Williams in "Cat on a Hot Tin Roof." Yet somehow, the truth of Mel Brooks's line in "The History of the World—Part I" cannot be concealed: "It's good to be the king."

"I'm going to take a bath."
"I'll alert the media."

ARTHUR

"Wherever there's a fight so hungry people can eat, I'll be there. Wherever there's a cop beatin' up a guy I'll be there."

THE GRAPES OF WRATH

"It's no shame to be poor, but it's no great honor either."

FIDDLER ON THE ROOF

"You should have done something before. Now he's too rich to kill."

GIANT

"The people—try and lick that!"

MEET JOHN DOE

"The farmers always win. We lose again."

THE MAGNIFICENT SEVEN

"We are so poor we don't even have a language. Just a stupid accent."

HISTORY OF THE WORLD—PART I

"We're in the money."

GOLD DIGGERS OF 1933

"Why do you live in a place like this when there are so many nice places to live?"
"Asthma."

MY MAN GODFREY
heiress to derelict

"It's good to be the king."

HISTORY OF THE WORLD—PART I

"My father left me forty million dollars. In those days that was a lot of money."

ANNIE

"The Gestapo would take away your Bloomingdale's charge card, you'd tell 'em everything."

ANNIE HALL

"His address is 49 East 49th Street, but he lives at the Ritz Bar."

THE AWFUL TRUTH

"I'm riding in an upper berth because staterooms are un-American."

THE PALM BEACH STORY

"We could make tens of thousands of dollars. More. We could make *thousands* of thousands of dollars."
"They call them millions."

ONCE UPON A TIME IN THE WEST

"You're the kind of man who would end the world's famine problem by having them all eat out."

CALIFORNIA SUITE

"All you need is twelve cashmere sweaters."

LORD LOVE A DUCK
entry requirements for an elitist high school club

"Prosperity is just around the corner."

MY MAN GODFREY
bum reassuring shantytown pal

"I wish I'd gone to Radcliffe too but Father wouldn't hear of it—he needed help behind the notions counter."

ALL ABOUT EVE

"My name is Howard Hughes."

MELVIN AND HOWARD

"I wish I had a dime for every dime I have."

ARTHUR

"Money's the only thing that ever saves you."

MRS. SOFFEL

"I know a lot of you are saying, what can I do? I'm just a little punk. I don't count. Well, you're dead wrong. The little punks have always counted because in the long run the character of a country is the sum total of its little punks."

MEET JOHN DOE

"We expect to lose a million next year, too. You know, Mr. Thatcher, at that rate of a million a year, we'll have to close this place—in sixty years."

CITIZEN KANE

"With the unrest in the world, I don't think anybody should have a yacht that sleeps more than twelve."

SOME LIKE IT HOT

"The rich and the beautiful sail to Lisbon. The poor are always with us."

CASABLANCA

"The rain people are people made of rain. And when they cry they disappear altogether."

THE RAIN PEOPLE

"Can't you make it just a little more? Please?"
"I'm sorry, madame. But diamonds are a drug on the market."

CASABLANCA

"It's no trick to make an awful lot of money if all you want is to make a lot of money."

CITIZEN KANE

"My religion? My dear, I'm a millionaire. That's my religion."

MAJOR BARBARA

"The fates, the destinies . . . they've been on me now nearly a quarter of a century. No letup. They said, 'Let him do without parents. He'll get along.' Then they decided, 'He doesn't need an education—that's for sissies.' And right at the beginning, they tossed a coin, heads he's poor, tails he's rich. So they tossed a coin— with two heads."

FOUR DAUGHTERS

"Big Daddy! Now what makes him so big? His big heart? His big belly? Or his big money?"

CAT ON A HOT TIN ROOF

"Look, when I say I want a whole floor, I don't want one wing and I don't want two wings. I want the whole bird."

BORN YESTERDAY

"It's always a pleasure to watch the rich enjoy the comforts of the poor."

GIGI

"The prettiest sight in this fine pretty world is the privileged class enjoying its privileges."

THE PHILADELPHIA STORY

"I have no curiosity about the working classes."

SEPARATE TABLES

"It doesn't matter who gives them as long as you never wear anything second-rate. Wait for the first-class jewels, Gigi. Hold on to your ideals."

GIGI

"I ain't dirty. I washed my face and hands before I came, I did."

PYGMALION

"I'll make you a little bet. Three times thirty-five is one hundred and five. I'll bet you one hundred and five thousand dollars you go to sleep before I do."

THE TREASURE OF THE SIERRA MADRE

"Look at me: I've worked myself up from nothing to a state of extreme poverty."

MONKEY BUSINESS

"I'm one of the undeserving poor. . . ."

MY FAIR LADY

"Have you ever been in love with poverty like Saint Francis? Have you ever been in love with dirt like Saint Simeon . . . ? Such passions are unnatural. This love of the common people may please an earl's granddaughter and a university professor, but I've been a poor man and a common man, and it has no romance for me."

MAJOR BARBARA

"Real diamonds! They must be worth their weight in gold."

SOME LIKE IT HOT

"A topaz? Among my jewels! Are you mad? It is a yellow diamond."

GIGI

"Personally, I think it is a bit tacky to wear diamonds before I'm forty."

BREAKFAST AT TIFFANY'S

"I had more fun in the back seat of a '39 Ford than I can ever have in the vault of the Chase National Bank."

BUTTERFIELD 8

"Leave it to the poor to pretend that poverty is a blessing."

MAJOR BARBARA

"That's what I like—everything done in contrasting shades of money."

THAT CERTAIN FEELING

"I think I could fix you up with Mr. Powell's chauffeur. The chauffeur has a very nice car, too."

STAGE DOOR

"Hunger is an indulgence with these peasants as gout is with us."

A TALE OF TWO CITIES

"I jes' trying to get on without shovin' anybody, that's all."

THE GRAPES OF WRATH

"One has to be as rich as you, Gaston, to be bored at Monte Carlo."

GIGI

"He's got dough, that's for sure. He bought Potters Island, the house for a million five cash . . . all in singles."

MURDER BY DEATH

"To most of you, your neighbor is a stranger, a guy with a barking dog and a fence around him. Now you can't be a stranger to any guy who's on your own team."

MEET JOHN DOE

"You sit around here and spin your little webs and think the whole world revolves around you and your money. Well, it doesn't, Mr. Potter."

IT'S A WONDERFUL LIFE

"I got so many maids some of the maids are taking care of the maids."

TITANIC

"Rich fellers come up. They die. Their kids ain't no good. And they die out. But we keep a-comin'. We're the people that live. Can't wipe us out. Can't lick us. We'll go on forever. 'Cause we're the people."

THE GRAPES OF WRATH

"You started out with nothing and you've really made something of yourself. Me? I started out in college with eight million dollars and I've still got eight million dollars. I just can't seem to get ahead."

PILLOW TALK

"You lose your manners when you're poor."

ANOTHER PART OF THE FOREST

"I've just been going over last month's bills and I find that you people have confused me with the Treasury Department."

MY MAN GODFREY

"Money seems to have lost its value these days. With two hundred thousand dollars my grandfather cornered the wheat market and started a panic in Omaha. Today you can't even frighten songwriters with it."

PILLOW TALK

"We got a little Spanish peasants' proverb: With the rich and mighty, always a little patience."

THE PHILADELPHIA STORY

"The wolf at the door? Why, I remember when it came right into my room and had pups."

SHE DONE HIM WRONG

"Money isn't all, you know. . . ."
"Not when you got it."

GIANT

CHAPTER
TWELVE

★

Drink

The movie censorship code kept a tight control on the display of drink and the behavior of drunkards. The censors were almost as strict about alcohol as they were about sex, which is saying quite a lot. This was a pity because the manifestations of drink have always proved to be rich in filmic material, whether comedic or dramatic. Mind you, though wretched excess in drink was forbidden, in virtually every movie, drinks were as ubiquitous as cigarettes. Someone was always sipping a highball or an Old Fashioned, and bibulous humor was common. "Why don't you get out of that wet coat and into a dry martini," wrote Sidney Sheldon in "The Major and the Minor." "She drove me to drink, that's the one thing I'm indebted to her for," wrote W.C. Fields in "Never Give a Sucker an Even Break." But excess in drink was to be avoided. The ravages of alcohol were sometimes explored, as in "The Lost Weekend" and "The Days of Wine and Roses," and its profits were examined in Prohibition gangster movies like "Public Enemy" and "Little Caesar." But drunkards could never be the object of approval, and intoxication could never be the subject of levity as it was years later in "Arthur" when the censors were gone. Who can forget Dudley Moore's offer to the harlot as he ushers her into his limousine: "We have cocaine, marijuana, vodka, gin, and some prune Danish."

"Even though a number of people have tried, no one has yet found a way to drink for a living."

THAT CERTAIN FEELING

"What is your nationality?"
"I'm a drunkard."

CASABLANCA

"Say when."
"Eight-thirty."

HISTORY OF THE WORLD—PART I

"I love him because he's the kind of guy that gets drunk on a glass of buttermilk."

BALL OF FIRE

"When I drink I'm very funny. At least that's what people tell me later."

ONLY WHEN I LAUGH

"Why don't you get out of that wet coat and into a dry martini?"

THE MAJOR AND THE MINOR

"Of all the gin joints in all the towns in all the world, she walks into mine."

CASABLANCA

"Now that's a smoo-oo-ooth drink."

ZIEGFELD FOLLIES

"Gimme a viskey. Ginger ale on the side. And don't be stingy, ba-bee."

ANNA CHRISTIE
Garbo's first words on film

"First drink of water he had in twenty years and then he had to get it by accident . . . How do you wire congratulations to the Pacific Ocean?"

A STAR IS BORN

"I wonder how many others there are like me—poor bedeviled guys on fire with thirst. Such comical figures to the rest of the world as they stagger blindly toward another binge . . ."

THE LOST WEEKEND

"This is the way I look when I'm sober. It's enough to make a person drink."

THE DAYS OF WINE AND ROSES

"Oh, my God! Someone's been sleeping in my dress."

MAME
an alcoholic rising from tub

"Champagne is a great levelerer—leveler. It makes you my equal."

THE PHILADELPHIA STORY

"I don't understand this conversation at all. How drunk am I?"

A LETTER TO THREE WIVES

"I like my conviction undiluted, same as I do my bourbon."

JEZEBEL

"Have a drink—just a little one to lessen the difference in our characters."

THE SCOUNDREL

"One's too many, and a hundred's not enough."

THE LOST WEEKEND

"Alcohol in the middle of the day is exciting when you're thirty and disastrous at seventy."

THE CHALK GARDEN

"Excuse me, folks. Somebody must have put alcohol in our liquor."

THE FIVE PENNIES

"I envy people who drink. At least they know what to blame everything on."

HUMORESQUE

"I am drunk. A wise man gets drunk to spend his time with fools."

FOR WHOM THE BELL TOLLS

"Honey, will you get me a Tab? My mouth is so dry they could shoot 'Lawrence of Arabia' in it."

THE LAST OF SHEILA

"Could you be persuaded to have a drink, dear?"
"Well, maybe just a tiny triple."

MAME

"You drank everything in this state. Try Nevada."

CALIFORNIA SUITE

"Well, you said you were looking for someone to do dramatic crimitism—criticism. I am drunk."

CITIZEN KANE

"Gin was mother's milk to her."

PYGMALION

"Hazel, you've got what is known in medicine as a hangover."

NOTHING SACRED

"I've had hangovers before, but this time even my hair hurts."

PILLOW TALK

"She drove me to drink. That's the one thing I'm indebted to her for."

NEVER GIVE A SUCKER AN EVEN BREAK

"I'm not a drinker—I'm a drunk."

THE LOST WEEKEND

"Bring a pitcher of beer every seven minutes until someone passes out, then bring one every ten minutes."

BACK TO SCHOOL

"It's cyanide cut with carbolic acid to give it a mellow flavor."

THE ICEMAN COMETH

"You were extremely attractive . . . but you were a little worse or better for wine—and there are rules about that."

THE PHILADELPHIA STORY

"We have a saying back in Texas, ma'am: 'Never drink anything stronger than you are—or older' "

PILLOW TALK

"I always start [drinking] around noon—in case it gets dark early."

PETE KELLY'S BLUES

"Here's mud in your throat."

SON OF PALEFACE

"You weren't born, you were squeezed out of a bar rag."

NEVER GIVE A SUCKER AN EVEN BREAK

"It's typical of my career that in the great crises of my life I should stand flanked by two incompetent alcoholics."

TWENTIETH CENTURY

"He's plastered."
"So are some of the finest erections in Europe."

MY FAVORITE YEAR

"Here's to plain speaking and clear understanding."

THE MALTESE FALCON

"To the Fountain of Trevi—to the lovely, romantic Fountain of Trevi where hope can be had for a penny."

THREE COINS IN THE FOUNTAIN

"To Reno, beautiful emblem of the great divide."

THE WOMEN

"A toast, Jedediah—to love on my terms. Those are the only terms anybody ever knows, his own."

CITIZEN KANE

"Would it be possible to just *rent* a couple of drinks?"

CALIFORNIA SUITE

"Do you tote a flask? You know, first aid to the nearly injured."

LADIES OF LEISURE

"The bartender is the aristocrat of the working class."

COCKTAIL

"You need a lot of drinks . . . to kill the bug that you have up your ass."

TERMS OF ENDEARMENT

"A lush can always find a reason. . . . If he's happy, he takes a couple of shots to celebrate his happiness. Sad, he needs 'em to drown his sorrow. Low, to pick him up. Excited, to calm him down. Sick, for his health. And healthy, it can't hurt."

COME FILL THE CUP

"How many gin and tonics have you had?"
"Three gins, one tonic."

CALIFORNIA SUITE

CHAPTER THIRTEEN

★

Marriage

Hollywood has never been famous for the longevity of its marriages. Hollywood is the place where for her last wedding, one actress arranged a quiet affair and only invited the immediate ex-husbands. The place where a sentimental star got divorced in the same dress in which her mother got divorced. The place where every Christmas some stars get custody of their families long enough to tape a Christmas special. Hollywoodians have a somewhat cynical attitude toward the marital state. "Marriage is not a word but a sentence," said Mae West. "It was so cold I almost got married," said Shelley Winters. Given this jaundiced view and Hollywood's history of marital disaster, it is not surprising to find that a compendium of screenplay dialogue on the subject of marriage should have an overall tone of irony and skepticism. Lines from the scripts of Neil Simon, Billy Wilder, George Axelrod, Buck Henry, and William Goldman bristle with an anti-marital bias. And adaptations of the plays of Oscar Wilde and Edward Albee are nearly misogynistic. However, we also find much dialogue in defense of marriage in the films of Paddy Chayefsky, Frank Capra, Joe Mankiewicz, Francis Coppola, and James Brooks. So the movie-going public, which through most of the history of cinema has been middle-class and married, has gotten an ambivalent idea of marriage and has been left to judge the institution for itself.

"I was once married. Now I just lease."

BUDDY BUDDY

"I never want to marry. I just want to get divorced."

LOVE AND DEATH

"I'm not livin' with you. We occupy the same cage, that's all."

CAT ON A HOT TIN ROOF

"I was once so poor I didn't know where my next husband was coming from."

SHE DONE HIM WRONG

"You're a guy. Why would a guy want to marry a guy?"
"Security."

SOME LIKE IT HOT

"I'm your wife, dammit. If you can't work up a winter passion for me, the least I'll require is respect and allegiance."

NETWORK

"You see, girls, I've run off with one of your husbands."

A LETTER TO THREE WIVES

"Men marry because they are tired, women marry because they are curious, and both are disappointed."

THE PICTURE OF DORIAN GRAY

"What do you call it when you hate the woman you love?"
"A wife."

HOW TO MURDER YOUR WIFE

"You are not special enough to overcome a bad marriage."

TERMS OF ENDEARMENT

"Here are my keys, here's my American Express card, here's my Bloomingdale's credit card."

KRAMER VS. KRAMER

"I guess it's sort of like being married to a doctor."

SUPERMAN II
*Lois Lane about being wed
to Superman*

"Forgive me for mistrusting you . . . it's just that you have been a little distant these last twenty-nine years."

A FUNNY THING HAPPENED ON THE WAY TO THE FORUM

"I'm not going to hand my daughter to some newlywed."

THE HEARTBREAK KID

"Benjamin, will you drive me home please? My husband took the car."

THE GRADUATE

"Henry's bed is Henry's province. He can people it in sheep for all I care—and often does."

THE LION IN WINTER

"I don't want to get married ever to anyone! You understand that? I want to do what *I* want to do!"

IT'S A WONDERFUL LIFE

"I don't believe it. No man with that awful wife and those ugly children can be anything but normal."

THE BEST MAN

"Write me a play about a nice, normal woman who shoots her husband."

ALL ABOUT EVE

"It was an abortion, like our marriage is an abortion, something unholy and evil."

THE GODFATHER

"In Rhode Island people do not remain engaged for fourteen years. They get married."
"So how come it's such a small state?"

GUYS AND DOLLS

"My wife and I—why, I never even knew her."
"How did the three children come, United Parcel?"

CACTUS FLOWER

"We're all dying, all the husbands and all the wives."

THE MISFITS

"I think you're rotten."
"I think you're swell so long as I'm not your husband."

DOUBLE INDEMNITY

"I'm not dying. Who said anything about dying? I want out of this marriage."

THE HEARTBREAK KID

"Now we're engaged."

THE LAST EMPEROR
after sucking her toes and putting a ring on one of them

"I've been married for forty years and I don't regret a day of it. The one day I don't regret is August 2, 1936; my wife was visiting her ailing mother."

HOW TO MURDER YOUR WIFE

"Five thousand pounds a year and not married. That's the most cheering piece of news since the Battle of Waterloo."

JANE EYRE

"How dear of you to let me out of jail."
"It's only for the holidays."

THE LION IN WINTER

"Why do you keep saying forty or fifty years? We're not even out of Georgia yet."

THE HEARTBREAK KID

"We were a very good marriage. Everyone said so, and not just the magazines, even our friends."

RICH AND FAMOUS

"How should I feel? I eat with a liar. I sleep with a liar. I make love to a liar."

THE WOMAN NEXT DOOR

"What did they do to make him get married this time? Stick a cannon up his ass?"

THE MARRYING MAN

"Why did you two ever get married?"
"I don't know. It was raining and we were in Pittsburgh."

THE BRIDE WALKS OUT

"I understand you want to marry my wife."

SLEUTH

"Buried three of 'em. Good women, bad diets."

HARRY AND TONTO

"I'm sorry that I was late, but I was busy trying to make a living. Okay?"

KRAMER VS. KRAMER

"Bad table manners have broken up more households than infidelity."

GIGI

"Marriage is like a dull meal, with the dessert at the beginning."

MOULIN ROUGE

"I'm more or less particular about whom my wife marries."

HIS GIRL FRIDAY

"How dare he make love to me and not be a married man?"

INDISCREET

"Stand still, Godfrey. It'll all be over in a minute."

MY MAN GODFREY
at his wedding ceremony

"You mustn't think too harshly of my secretaries. They were kind and understanding when I came to the office after a hard day at home."

MR. SKEFFINGTON

"What most wives fail to realize is that their husbands' philandering has nothing whatever to do with them."

THE PHILADELPHIA STORY

"The first man that can think up a good explanation how he can be in love with his wife and another woman is going to win that prize they're always giving in Sweden."

THE WOMEN

"When a marriage goes on the rocks, the rocks are there—right there."

CAT ON A HOT TIN ROOF
slapping a bed

"Are you a critic or a wife?"

THE COUNTRY GIRL

"To my darling wife, Leon, whom I love more than any man has loved another man in all eternity . . ."

DOG DAY AFTERNOON

"I just couldn't go to heaven without Clare. Why, I get lonesome for him even when I go to Ohio."

LIFE WITH FATHER

"Ain't much difference between kidnapping and marrying. You get snatched from your parents—but in marriage nobody offers a reward."

THE BRIDE CAME C.O.D.

"When you've been married to a woman for twelve years, you don't just sit down at the breakfast table and say, 'Pass the sugar—and I want a divorce.' "

THE APARTMENT

"I married your mother because I wanted children. Imagine my disappointment when you arrived."

HORSE FEATHERS

"One day when I was about six, my parents had a row, and my mother—she threw a pickled herring at my dad and missed. It splattered all against the wall. I took one look at that pickled herring, and that's when I decided to become an abstract expressionist."

AN UNMARRIED WOMAN

"That's the only good thing about divorce. You get to sleep with your mother."

THE WOMEN

"It offends my vanity to have anyone who was even remotely my wife remarry so obviously beneath her."

THE PHILADELPHIA STORY

"What did you think I was anyway? A guy that walks into a good-looking dame's front parlor and says, 'Good afternoon, I sell accident insurance on husbands.' "

DOUBLE INDEMNITY

"I now pronounce you men and wives."

SEVEN BRIDES FOR SEVEN BROTHERS

"You know, I don't believe Clare has come right out and told me he loves me since we've been married. 'Course, I know he does because I keep reminding him of it."

LIFE WITH FATHER

"He married for love . . . that's why he did everything. That's why he went into politics. It seems we weren't enough. He wanted all the voters to love him, too."

CITIZEN KANE

"Tell me why it is that every man who seems attractive these days is either married or barred on a technicality."

GENTLEMEN'S AGREEMENT

"I believe that a man is fire and a woman fuel. And she who is born beautiful is born married."

VIVA ZAPATA!

"I wanted to marry her when I saw the moonlight shining on the barrel of her father's shotgun."

OKLAHOMA!

"Make him feel important. If you do that, you'll have a happy and wonderful marriage—like two out of every ten couples."

BAREFOOT IN THE PARK

"There is nothing so nice as a new marriage. No psychosis yet, no regressions. No deep complexes . . ."

SPELLBOUND

"You know how them big, strong, redheaded men are: They just got to get to the point. So we got married . . . I ain't had no chance to think about love since."

THE WOMEN

"Marriage is not forbidden to us, but instead of getting married at once, it sometimes happens we get married at last."

GIGI

"What difference does it make who you marry—so long as he's a southerner and thinks like you?"

GONE WITH THE WIND

"Before a man gets married he's like a tree in the forest. He stands there independent . . . and then he's chopped down. His branches are cut off and he's stripped of his bark and he's thrown into the river with the rest of the logs."

PILLOW TALK

"If my father was the head of our house, my mother was its heart."

How Green Was My Valley

"I never dated Carlo. I married him. I never dated him."

Auntie Mame

"My mother and father together are like a bad car wreck."

Dog Day Afternoon

"I was married for nine years. Eight of those years were very passionate . . . Passion's a mild word for it really. It was more like war."

An Unmarried Woman

"I'm not going to marry anyone who says, 'You gotta marry me, Howard.' . . . She can at least say 'please.' "
"Please marry me, Howard."

Picnic

"Marry me and I'll never look at another horse."

A Day at the Races

"[She] married a Polish chess player who committed suicide after losing three hundred matches in a row."

Murder by Death

"I didn't marry any of them . . . they married me."

My Favorite Year

"Maybe you're sorry you married me now, Doc. You didn't know I was going to get old and fat and sloppy."

Come Back, Little Sheba

"I wear the pants and she beats me with the belt."

All My Sons

" 'Shut up'? You can't talk like that to me until after we're married."

Son of Paleface

"I want to be a Sadie . . . that's a married lady."

FUNNY GIRL

"Strange that a man can live with a woman for ten years and not know the first thing about her."

THE LETTER

"I'm a man, so I married. Wife, children, house, everything, the full catastrophe."

ZORBA THE GREEK

"My first wife was clever. My second was ambitious. My third . . . If you want to be happy marry a stupid woman."

THE PRIVATE LIFE OF HENRY VIII

"Success? That's a strange choice of words. Usually newlyweds are wished happiness."

FEMALE ON THE BEACH

"Oliver, if you marry her now, I'll not give you the time of day."
"Father, you don't know the time of day."

LOVE STORY

"I don't want somebody pointing at Joan and me in a couple of years, telling some miserable story ending with 'and they're still together.' "

LOVERS AND OTHER STRANGERS

"Everyone has trouble at home. The only ones who deny it have had too much of it."

THE COUNTRY GIRL

"Truth is pain and sweat and paying bills and making love to a woman that you don't love anymore."

CAT ON A HOT TIN ROOF

"As many times as I'll be married, I'll never understand women."

PILLOW TALK

"I want you to be a merry widower."

LOVE STORY

"We've decided on a white wedding, in spite of the circumstances."

ROOM AT THE TOP

"Do you Alice, Ruth, Martha, Liza, Sarah, Dorcas, take these men to be your lawfully married husbands?"

SEVEN BRIDES FOR SEVEN BROTHERS

"One wife? One God, that I can understand—but one wife! That is not civilized. It is not generous."

BEN-HUR

"In the last analysis, nothing is any good unless you can look up or turn around in bed—and there he is."

ALL ABOUT EVE

"Are you still in the fight game?"
"In a way. I married Benjy's mother."

MY FAVORITE YEAR

"I live in a two-bedroom duplex in downtown Oakland. We have a 1948 Kaiser, a blonde three-piece dinette set, a Motorola TV, and we go bowling at least once a week. I mean, what else could anyone ask for?"

SAME TIME, NEXT YEAR

"Lovemaking is the red tape of marriage."

BLUEBEARD'S EIGHTH WIFE

"I must have your golden hair, fascinating smile, your lovely arms, your form divine—"
"Wait a minute! Is this a proposal or are you taking an inventory?"

BELLE OF THE NINETIES

"Why don't you get a divorce and settle down?"

HUMORESQUE

CHAPTER FOURTEEN

★

Horror and Fantasy

Horror films are not the ideal medium for the creative writer who loves the song of words rather than the sound of screams. But writers continue to write what audiences crave and studios demand. The horror genre was perhaps the first to appear in films and the one with the greatest longevity. Even today, when mammoth budgets bring to every kind of film the risk of financial horror at the box office, movie horror remains a popular option. The reason such films succeed is that they give moviegoers the delicious pleasures of terror. Writers and producers alike enjoy creating horror flicks because they are impervious to the critics. Reviewers may trash or ignore them, but audiences continue to come. Though horror films are remembered more often for the savagery of their images than the elegance of their prose, sometimes a line emerges that remains with us. Here is a brief medley of remembered lines from the horror and fantasy species.

"It's alive!"

FRANKENSTEIN

"I'm sorry, Dave, I'm afraid I can't do that."

2001: A SPACE ODYSSEY

"It was beauty killed the beast."

KING KONG

"I never drink . . . wine."

DRACULA

"I'll get you, my pretty, and your little dog too."

THE WIZARD OF OZ

"You're going to die up there."

THE EXORCIST

"Welcome to Bates Motel."

PSYCHO

"He meddled in things men should leave alone."

THE INVISIBLE MAN

"I'll hurt you if you stay."

THE FLY

"I'll be back."

THE TERMINATOR

"They're coming! They're coming!"

INVASION OF THE BODY SNATCHERS

"Feed me! Feed me!"

LITTLE SHOP OF HORRORS

"What have you done with his eyes!"

ROSEMARY'S BABY

"Don't get him wet, keep him away from bright light, and never *never* feed him after midnight."

GREMLINS

"I realize I don't look so hot, but I thought you'd be glad to see me."

AN AMERICAN WEREWOLF IN LONDON
*returning in ghoulish state
of decomposition*

"We're all afraid of the dark inside ourselves."

HALLOWEEN II

"He slimed me."

GHOSTBUSTERS

"Take him to the Shock Tower."

THE ADVENTURES OF BUCKAROO BANZAI

"Tell me more about the places you'll show me where the jackals eat—'21.'"

SHEENA

"I'm a mean, green mother from outer space."

LITTLE SHOP OF HORRORS

"I am Dracula. I bid you welcome."

DRACULA

"We'll start with a few murders. Big men. Little men. Just to show we make no distinctions."

THE INVISIBLE MAN

"It's sad when a mother has to speak the words to condemn her own son, but I couldn't allow them to believe that I would commit murder."

PSYCHO

"Every night when the moon is full, I turn into a wolf."
"You and fifty million other guys."

ABBOTT AND COSTELLO MEET FRANKENSTEIN

"I know you have a civil tongue in your head—I sewed it there myself."

I WAS A TEENAGE FRANKENSTEIN

"Pardon me, boy, is this the Transylvania Station?"

YOUNG FRANKENSTEIN

"Let them see what kind of person I am. I'm not even going to swat that fly."

PSYCHO

"Snakes—why does it always have to be snakes?"

RAIDERS OF THE LOST ARK

"E. T. phone home."

E.T. THE EXTRA-TERRESTRIAL

"We came, we saw, we kicked its ass."

GHOSTBUSTERS

"I have one question, Dr. Frankenstein."
"That's Fronkonsteen!"

YOUNG FRANKENSTEIN

"Get away from her, you bitch."

ALIENS

"Listen to them. Children of the night. What music they make."

DRACULA
on howling wolves

"A greater hive of scum and villainy you will not find elsewhere in the galaxy."

STAR WARS

"Why do we always expect them to come in metal ships?"

INVASION OF THE BODY SNATCHERS

"The worm is the spice."

DUNE

"I'm a rather brilliant surgeon. Perhaps I can help you with that hump."
"What hump?"

YOUNG FRANKENSTEIN

"Stop, Dave. Will you stop? I'm afraid, Dave. My mind is going . . . I can feel it. I can feel it . . . There is no question about it."

2001: A SPACE ODYSSEY

CHAPTER FIFTEEN

★

Farce

What has happened to farce today? In the thirties and forties there were the Marx Brothers, Chaplin, W.C. Fields, and Mae West. There were the plays of Kaufman and Hart. There was the writing of S.J. Perelman, Robert Benchley, and Arthur Kober. Where do we turn for farce today? "Saturday Night Live" and the movies of their alumni? The columns of Dave Barry, Art Buchwald, and Lewis Grizzard? The monologues of Johnny Carson, Jay Leno, and Mark Russell? The Top Ten Lists of David Letterman? Thanks to the technology of VCRs and your local video shop, we can enjoy the films of the Brothers Marx, Buster Keaton, Laurel and Hardy, and the rest. But farce, unlike revenge, is not a dish that is best when served cold. Who is writing farce today for the screen? Woody Allen, whose farcical "Bananas" and "Take the Money and Run" were such exemplary examples of the species, has deserted this genre for more substantial work. Mel Brooks, after the riotous "Blazing Saddles" and "Young Frankenstein," has declined to "Life Stinks." Preston Sturges has gone to his reward and the writers of the Crosby-Hope road pictures cannot relate to teenage audiences. Occasionally, an "Arthur" or "A

Fish Called Wanda'' or Neil Simon's ''The Cheap Detective'' arrives to remind us how amusing comedy can be. But for the most part, farce, like the Broadway show tune, is a genre lost in time. Here are some lines to remind us of just how funny farce can be.

''One morning I shot an elephant in my pajamas. How he got in my pajamas I don't know.''

DUCK SOUP

''But you don't understand. I'm a man.''
''Well, nobody's perfect.''

SOME LIKE IT HOT

''A toon killed my brother.''

WHO FRAMED ROGER RABBIT

''Separate checks?''

HISTORY OF THE WORLD—PART I
waiter to apostles at Last Supper

''Either this man is dead or my watch has stopped.''

A DAY AT THE RACES

''I don't have a photograph, but you can have my footprints. They're upstairs in my socks.''

MONKEY BUSINESS

''I'll write the *O* now and fill in the *K* later.''

A DAY AT THE RACES
man signing memo

''Yes, Lord, I will pass on unto thy people your fifteen . . . er . . . ten commandments.''

HISTORY OF THE WORLD—PART I
Moses dropping tablet

''Who are you going to believe—me or your own eyes?''

A DAY AT THE RACES

"The pellet with the poison's in the vessel with the pestle, has the brew that is true."

THE COURT JESTER

"I could dance with you until the cows come home. On second thought, I'd rather dance with the cows till you come home."

DUCK SOUP

"They're not going to torture me. It hurts."

ROAD TO BALI

"Anything further, Father? That can't be right. Isn't it, 'Anything Father, further?' "

HORSE FEATHERS

"I don't mind being killed, but I resent hearing it from a character whose head comes to a point."

A NIGHT IN CASABLANCA

"In studying your basic metabolism, we first listen to your heartbeat. And if your hearts beat anything but diamonds and clubs, it's because your partner is cheating."

HORSE FEATHERS

"Was 1 a good year?"

A FUNNY THING HAPPENED ON THE WAY TO THE FORUM

"As Chairwoman of the Reception Committee, I welcome you with open arms."
"Is that so? How late do you stay open?"

DUCK SOUP

"You may call me Tanka."
"Tanka?"
"You're welcome."

ROBERTA

"You're awfully shy for a lawyer."
"You bet I'm shy. I'm a shyster lawyer."

MONKEY BUSINESS

"It's the old, old story. 'Boy Meets Girl'—'Romeo and Juliet'—'Minneapolis and St. Paul.' "

"This is the screwiest picture I was ever in."

ROAD TO MOROCCO

"Chicolinni here may talk like an idiot and look like an idiot, but don't let that fool you. He really is an idiot."

DUCK SOUP

"Oh, why can't we break away from all this, just you and I, and lodge with my fleas in the hills—I mean, flee to my lodge in the hills."

MONKEY BUSINESS

"You're a disgrace to our family name of Wagstaff, if such a thing is possible."

HORSE FEATHERS

"These woods give me the creeps. It reminds me of the moors of Scotland."

"No, no, darling. The Moores have a beach house."

MURDER BY DEATH

"I am troubled by insomnia."

"Well, I know a good cure for it . . . Get plenty of sleep."

NEVER GIVE A SUCKER AN EVEN BREAK

"COME AHEAD STOP STOP BEING A SAP STOP YOU CAN EVEN BRING ALBERTO STOP MY HUSBAND IS STOPPING AT YOUR HOTEL STOP WHEN DO YOU START STOP"

TOP HAT

"Of course, you all know who De Soto was. He discovered a body of water. You've all heard of the water that they named after him: De Soto Water."

THE COCOANUTS

"How do you expect me to sell a half-eaten hot dog?"
"First you insult me. Then you ask me for my advice regarding salesmanship."

NEVER GIVE A SUCKER AN EVEN BREAK

"Not many people come to the manor these days. It's nice to hear people again."

MURDER BY DEATH
blind butler reminiscing

"You can cry on my shoulder. I'm not going to bathe anyway."

STAGE DOOR

"Don't get saucy with me, Bernaise."

HISTORY OF THE WORLD—PART I

"Princess? Did you say 'princess,' Arthur?"
"Yes. There is a *very* small country . . . Rhode Island could beat the crap out of it in a war . . . It's eighty-five cents in a cab from one end of the country to the other. I'm talking small."

ARTHUR

"Running a sanitarium takes a man of peculiar talents."
"I've got some of the most peculiar talents you'll ever find."

A DAY AT THE RACES

"It's one for all and it's three for five."

THE THREE MUSKETEERS

"Henderson, Mayo, '22."
"Harper, Johns Hopkins, '28."
"Quackenbush, Dodge, '36."

A DAY AT THE RACES

CHAPTER
SIXTEEN

★

Women

American movies have always reflected the biases of American screenwriters toward women. Scenarists presented women either as saints or whores, Madonnas or harlots. Oh, yes, there were a few female screenwriters— Anita Luce and Lillian Hellman and Nora Ephron—whose views were more realistic. But most of the screenwriters were men. And their often chauvinistic, misogynistic attitudes shone through in the female characters they painted in their screenplays. So when characters spoke of women, when they characterized them, praised them, damned them, there was an underlying feeling in the dialogue that women were either to be worshipped or despised. Those were the two inevitable roles in which female actresses were cast: Pola Negri or Ingrid Bergman, Gloria Grahame or Jennifer Jones. But if America's screenwriters were sometimes guilty of slandering or idealizing women, their talents were so diverse that their movies presented a splendidly disparate portrait. Moviegoers came to see women through the eyes of such men as Woody Allen, Clifford Odets, Truman Capote, Billy Wilder, F. Scott Fitzgerald, John Huston, Julius and Philip Epstein, Tennessee Williams, Stanley Shapiro, and Garson Kanin. Movie moguls realized that the most marketable "product" they had to sell was women—in their saintly or sexual embodiments. So, whenever in doubt, if they wanted to bring out the audiences, they would push the reliable button marked "Women."

"They all start out as Juliets and wind up as Lady Macbeths."

THE COUNTRY GIRL

"I guess you could say I'm half saint, half whore."
"Here's hoping I get the half that eats."

LOVE AND DEATH

"I keep my undies in the icebox."

THE SEVEN YEAR ITCH

"Not much meat on her but what's there is choice."

PAT AND MIKE

"You're a professional virgin."

THE MOON IS BLUE

"No woman can look good at five o'clock in the afternoon—except possibly Tatum O'Neal."

CALIFORNIA SUITE

"Let's spend one night talking to someone with higher voices than us."

THE ODD COUPLE

"All the elements in the human body are worth one dollar and ninety-eight cents."
"I'll take fifty dollars worth."

GIRL HAPPY

"I like a woman who can cook and sew and clean."
"And weave."

THE PALM BEACH STORY

"Hush, dear, Mother's fighting."

THE LION IN WINTER

"I'm twenty-six, and I'm single, and I'm a school teacher, and that's the bottom of the pit."

BUTCH CASSIDY AND THE SUNDANCE KID

"Are you an adventuress?"

"Of course I am. All women are. We have to be."

THE LADY EVE

"If a guy doesn't have a doll, who would holler on him?"

GUYS AND DOLLS

"Every time I see a pregnant woman I want to greet her as a friend, a conspirator."

GUNS IN THE TREES

"She's half angel, half siren, all woman."

JEZEBEL

"Grand Central Station and step on it, darling!"

BREAKFAST AT TIFFANY'S

"I couldn't go through with it. I left. Walked out."

"You mean you wasted a stewardess?"

CACTUS FLOWER

"Girls! Girls! Hello girls! Would the more attractive of you please step forward?"

ARTHUR

"Look how she moves—it's like Jell-O on springs . . . I tell you it's a whole different sex."

SOME LIKE IT HOT

"Why the hell do men get better looking as they get older? Remind me to bring it up to the Equal Rights Commission."

CALIFORNIA SUITE

"I wonder why Mama hung herself."

"I don't know. She had a bad day."

CRIMES OF THE HEART

"I'm like the earth, old man, there isn't any way around me."

THE LION IN WINTER

"I've been things and seen places."

SHE DONE HIM WRONG

"My body temperature is one hundred degrees."

BODY HEAT

"I feel safer than a virgin at a eunuch convention."

MARRIED TO THE MOB

"You bought the new girdles a size smaller. I can feel it."

ALL ABOUT EVE

"I'd like to get that broad in a bowling alley."

CONTINENTAL DIVIDE

"There's a name for you ladies, but it isn't used in high society—outside of a kennel."

THE WOMEN

"Women represent the triumph of mind over matter just as men represent the triumph of mind over morals."

THE PICTURE OF DORIAN GRAY

"Certain women should be struck regularly, like gongs."

PRIVATE LIVES

"There are two kinds of women: those who pay too much attention to themselves and those who don't pay enough."

THE COUNTRY GIRL

"Why is it that women always think they understand men better than men do?"
"Maybe because they live with them."

THE COUNTRY GIRL

"When it comes to women, you're a true democrat."

CASABLANCA

"Are you a man of good character where women are concerned?"
"Have you ever known a man of good character where women are concerned?"

PYGMALION

"I just got your call. I was having a manicure."
"At two o'clock in the morning?"
"I cannot sleep with long fingernails."

SILK STOCKINGS

"Life with Mary was like being in a phone booth with an open umbrella. No matter which way you turned, you got it in the eye."

THAT CERTAIN FEELING

"She tried to sit on my lap while I was standing up."

THE BIG SLEEP

"We must beware of these men. They're desperate characters. Not one of them looked at my legs."

BEAT THE DEVIL

"I hate this dress. My husband says I look as though I were going to sing in it."

THE WOMEN

"I was reading a book the other day. The guy said that machinery is going to take the place of every profession."
"Oh, my dear. That's something you need never worry about."

DINNER AT EIGHT

"This is very unusual. I've never been alone with a man before—even with my dress on. With my dress off, it's most unusual."

ROMAN HOLIDAY

"I am Tondelayo."

WHITE CARGO

"Can you go for a doctor?"
"Sure, send him in."

LOVE ME TONIGHT

"I get so tired of being told I'm pretty."

PICNIC

"A kiss on the hand might feel very good, but a diamond tiara lasts forever."

GENTLEMEN PREFER BLONDES

"How did you get into that dress—with a spray gun?"

ROAD TO RIO

"You're like an old coat that's hanging in his closet. Every time he reaches in, there you are. Don't be there once."

THE DESK SET

"I used to go with a girl who read books. She joined the Book of the Month Club, and they had her reading books all the time. She had no more finished one than they'd shoot her another."

PICNIC

"Take an editorial. 'To the women of America. . . . Banish the black, burn the blue, and bury the beige. From now on, girls, think pink!' "

FUNNY FACE

"These girls in love never realize they should be honestly dishonest instead of being dishonestly honest."

THREE COINS IN THE FOUNTAIN

"John, where did you learn so much about women's clothes?"
"My mother wore women's clothes."

A FOREIGN AFFAIR

"Most girls would give their eyes for a chance to see Monte."
"Wouldn't that rather defeat the purpose?"

REBECCA

"She's a phony, but she's a *real* phony, know what I mean, kid?"

BREAKFAST AT TIFFANY'S

"They tell me in Paris, if you don't buy your gown from Roberta, you're not dressed at all."
"I see—nude if you don't, and nude if you do."

ROBERTA

"Do you know what I feel like? I feel all the time like a cat on a hot tin roof."

CAT ON A HOT TIN ROOF

"I'm not sure she's capable of any real feeling. She's the television generation. She learned life from Bugs Bunny."

NETWORK

"A girl can't get married without a permanent. It wouldn't be legal."

FOUR DAUGHTERS

"In my time, women with hair like that didn't come outside in the daylight."

GO WEST, YOUNG MAN

"Women should be kept illiterate and clean, like canaries."

WOMAN OF THE YEAR

"Queen Cleopatra is widely read, well versed in the natural sciences and mathematics. She speaks seven languages proficiently. Were she not a woman, one would consider her to be an intellectual."

CLEOPATRA

"One woman should never judge another. She hasn't the glands for it."

QUO VADIS

"I am Mata Hari, my own master."

MATA HARI

"Your wife is safe with Tonetti—he prefers spaghetti."

THE GAY DIVORCEE

"If I'd forgotten myself with that girl, I'd remember it."

TOP HAT

"Too many girls follow the line of least resistance."
"Yeah, but a good line is hard to resist."

KLONDIKE ANNIE

"She's got those eyes that run up and down men like a searchlight."

THE WOMEN

"Does this boat go to Europe, France?"

GENTLEMEN PREFER BLONDES

"I am not part of your luggage. Whatever I am, I am not part of your luggage."

SWEET BIRD OF YOUTH

"My understanding of women goes only as far as the pleasures."

ALFIE

"She cut off her nipples with a garden shears. You call that normal?"

REFLECTIONS IN A GOLDEN EYE

"Just because you have good manners doesn't mean I suddenly turn into Dale Evans."

ALICE DOESN'T LIVE HERE ANYMORE

"I'm not bad, I'm just drawn that way."

WHO FRAMED ROGER RABBIT

"Sometimes I sing and dance around my house in my underwear. That doesn't make me Madonna."

WORKING GIRL

"She is playing solitaire with her memories."

ANASTASIA

"If there's one thing I know, it's men. I ought to. It's been my life's work."

DINNER AT EIGHT

"There's a guy who never goes out of a girl's mind. He just stays there like a heavy meal."

THE BACHELOR AND THE BOBBY-SOXER

"It would take a great woman to make Crassus fall out of love with himself."

SPARTACUS

"Here, take my handkerchief. Never at any crisis in your life have I known you to have a handkerchief."

GONE WITH THE WIND

"It's too bad I'm not covering this dinner of yours tonight because I've got an angle that would really be sensational: The outstanding woman of the year isn't a woman at all."

WOMAN OF THE YEAR

"Who the hell do you think you're dealing with? In case you didn't happen to notice it . . . I'm one helluva gorgeous chick."

MIDNIGHT COWBOY

"When you call me madam, smile."

CALL ME MADAM

"He did a whole series of nudes of me. It's a funny feeling to know you're being hung naked in some stranger's living room."

HANNAH AND HER SISTERS

"Do you know how an ugly woman feels? Do you know what it is to be ugly all your life and to feel in here that you are beautiful?"

FOR WHOM THE BELL TOLLS

"You see, Mr. Scott, in the water I'm a very skinny lady."

THE POSEIDON ADVENTURE

"Cry? I never knew a woman that size had that much water in her."

PILLOW TALK

"Women . . . inspire us with the desire to do masterpieces and always prevent us from carrying them out."

THE PICTURE OF DORIAN GRAY

"Funny business, a woman's career. The things you drop on your way up the ladder so you can move faster. You forget you'll need them again when you're back to being a woman."

ALL ABOUT EVE

"Women act like men and want to be treated like women."

AN AMERICAN IN PARIS

"Women make the best psychoanalysts till they fall in love. After that, they make the best patients."

SPELLBOUND

"A woman can muck up a hunt party. They get bored. They don't like killing. They get lazy. Still, they want their money's worth."

THE MACOMBER AFFAIR

"When women go wrong, men go right after them."

SHE DONE HIM WRONG

"Even as a kid, I always went for the wrong woman. . . . When my mother took me to see 'Snow White,' everyone fell in love with Snow White. I immediately fell for the wicked queen."

TAKE THE MONEY AND RUN

"There was a maharajah who came all the way from India to beg for one of her silk stockings to strangle himself with."

SUNSET BOULEVARD

"It's the wonderful way they smell. I told my wife I would never look at another woman if I could cut off my nose."

"What did she say?"

"She said I was aiming too high."

SWEET LIBERTY

"She only said 'no' once—and then she couldn't hear the question."

42ND STREET

"I like a man who can run faster than I can."

GENTLEMEN PREFER BLONDES

"Have you heard the one about the girl tuba player that was stranded on a desert island with a one-legged jockey?"

SOME LIKE IT HOT

"There are women who reach a perfect time of life, when the face will never again be as good, the body as graceful or powerful. It had happened that year to Julia."

JULIA

"A pretty girl doesn't have long—just a few years. Then she's the equal of kings. She can walk out of a shanty like this and live in a palace."

PICNIC

"Why can't a woman be more like a man?"

MY FAIR LADY

CHAPTER
SEVENTEEN

★

Westerns

For a screenwriter to write effective dialogue for a Western was like bringing a sandwich to a banquet. The traditional means of expression of a cowboy star called for a minimum of words and a maximum of silent nobility. This worked out fine for stars like Steve McQueen and Clint Eastwood who are not at their best when burdened with heavy dialogue. Their forte is undertones, scowls, and body language. But even where the star could deliver lines—Gary Cooper, Gregory Peck, or William Holden— the scenarist provided little in the way of expressive speech. There were exceptions to this rule of wordlessness on the range (where seldom was heard an intelligent word). Henry Fonda spoke some indelible lines in "The Ox-Bow Incident," and William Goldman gave some memorable lines to Newman and Redford in "Butch Cassidy and the Sundance Kid." But generally, the dialogue in Westerns could as easily be mumbled to a horse. The film's appeal was intended to be found in the conflict between good and evil. Perhaps the most unforgettable lines in a Western were those of Mel Brooks and his cadre of screenwriters in his inspired sendup of the genre in "Blazing Saddles." Who can forget the scene in which rednecks shout at the railroad workers: "How about a good old nigger work song?" And the men respond with a chorus of "I Get a Kick Out of You."

"Who *are* those guys?"

BUTCH CASSIDY AND THE SUNDANCE KID

"They're makin' me run. I've never run from anybody before."

HIGH NOON

"Who was that masked man?"

LEGEND OF THE LONE RANGER

"I hear you're a man with true grit."

TRUE GRIT

"It's the first time I rode shotgun for a hearse."

THE MAGNIFICENT SEVEN

"That ain't right. I've had enough of what ain't right."

SILVERADO

"I'm not a sore loser or anything, but when we're done, if I'm dead, kill him."

BUTCH CASSIDY AND THE SUNDANCE KID

"How can you trust a man who wears a belt and suspenders? Man doesn't even trust his pants."

ONCE UPON A TIME IN THE WEST

"Get up, you scum-sucking pig or I'll tear your hands off."

ONE-EYED JACKS

"When you goin' to shoot, don't talk, shoot."

THE GOOD, THE BAD AND THE UGLY

"Excuse me while I whip this out."

BLAZING SADDLES

"Next time I say let's go someplace like Bolivia, let's go someplace like Bolivia."

BUTCH CASSIDY AND THE SUNDANCE KID

"We're after *men*—and I wish to God I was with them!"

THE WILD BUNCH

"So you've found you're not a businessman after all."
"Just a man."
"An ancient race."

ONCE UPON A TIME IN THE WEST

"Well, come see a fat old man sometime."

TRUE GRIT

"Did you bring a horse for me?"
"Well, looks like we're shy one horse."
"No, you brought two too many."

ONCE UPON A TIME IN THE WEST

"I don't think America is ashamed of Jesse James . . .
Maybe it's because he was so good at what he was
doing."

JESSE JAMES

"Damn it all, why is everything we're good at illegal?"

BUTCH CASSIDY AND THE SUNDANCE KID

"I've talked with the prisoner. He's a friend of Lily
Langtry's. It stands to reason no friend of Lily Langtry
goes around stealing horses . . ."

THE WESTERNER

"Poker is played by desperate men who cherish money.
I don't lose because I have nothing to lose, including
my life."

GUNFIGHT AT THE O.K. CORRAL

"Just how big a coward are you?"
"Well, I was captain of the Olympic team."

SON OF PALEFACE

"I can tell you what an Indian will do to you, but not a
woman."

THE PLAINSMAN

"Resistance is going to be a darn sight harder for you than for females protected by the shape of sows."

DUEL IN THE SUN

"Does she smile when you mount her?"

LITTLE BIG MAN

"I myself never surrendered. But they got my horse, and *it* surrendered."

THE OUTLAW JOSIE WALES

CHAPTER
EIGHTEEN

★

Youth and
Children

S tudio executives, and the directors, producers, and
stars they employ to create today's movies, are aston-
ishingly young. This is because today's moviegoers are
young and the conventional wisdom teaches that the young
have a better understanding of the tastes of youth. This is
why filmmakers like Frank Capra and John Huston had
terrible trouble finding films to direct during the later years
of their lives. Even gifted movie makers like Peter Bogdanovich and William Friedkin find themselves somewhat
over the hill at a surprisingly early age. Most movies
today are created by the young, and their subject is youth.
Yesterday's screenwriters were not quite as green as today's, since their target audience was the family. This was
before the coming of television after which movies became
a dating device, and parents and grandparents got their
"B" movies for free on the tube and their "A" movies a
few months after they opened. Today, when screenwriters
write of youth they write from the perspective of the young.
Yesterday's screenwriters wrote of youth through the im-
perfect prism of memory. Here are some of the more
memorable lines from the movies of yesterday and today
on the subject of youth and children. It is interesting to

observe the varying perceptions of Hollywood screenwriters during an era when movies are written by the young for the young, as opposed to the era when they were written by the not-so-young for everyone.

"I wish I were . . . big."

BIG

"What are you rebelling against?"
"Whadaya got?"

THE WILD ONES

"I never had any friends later on like the ones I had when I was twelve. Jesus, does anyone?"

STAND BY ME

"My mother died when I was six. My father raped me when I was twelve."
"So you had six relatively good years."

ARTHUR

"It's economically unsound to grow up."

NOTHING IN COMMON

"Henry, I have a confession—I don't much like our children."

THE LION IN WINTER

"You better go to your room."
"This is a one-room apartment."

A THOUSAND CLOWNS

"You're tearing me apart!"

REBEL WITHOUT A CAUSE

"Josh can sing all the words to that detergent commercial."
"That's great. Two more years he'll have high triglycerides."

ANNIE HALL

"Form a circle, boys on the outside, girls on the inside."
"Where will you be?"

WEST SIDE STORY

"Surf's up!"

BEACH PARTY

"What about killing the first born male child in each household. No, that's been done."

BLAZING SADDLES

"It's unavoidable. When you grow up, your heart dies."

THE BREAKFAST CLUB

"Maybe it's a mistake to feel sorry for kids like that. Then, maybe it's a mistake not to."

KITTEN WITH A WHIP

"The boy keeps wondering if your promises are any good."
"There's no sense wondering if the air is good if there's nothing else to breathe."

THE LION IN WINTER

"The FBI is wrong in reporting to you that I have no children. Ideas are my children and I have hundreds of them."

FIRST MONDAY IN OCTOBER

"You have a lot to learn—and I hope you never learn it."

HARVEY

"If I'd get back my youth, I'd do anything in the world—except get up early, take exercise or be respectable."

THE PICTURE OF DORIAN GRAY

"Adolescence is a time when people worry about things there's no need to worry about."

SHIP OF FOOLS

"You suffer from the critical disease of being young. The Lord deliver me from ever having to go through that again."

THE GREEN YEARS

"I'm afraid I was born a hundred years before my time."
"I was born ten days ahead of mine."

AH, WILDERNESS!

"The baby arrived three minutes ahead of schedule, so Mr. Pendergast refused delivery."

THE MORE THE MERRIER

"Children are life renewing itself, Captain Butler. And when life does that, danger seems very unimportant."

GONE WITH THE WIND

" . . . alligators have the right idea. They eat their young."

MILDRED PIERCE

"If I was married to you three years . . . you'd have three kids already and the fourth in the oven."

CAT ON A HOT TIN ROOF

"Peggy, you know what a penis is—stay away from it."

PEGGY SUE GOT MARRIED

"I always thought I could give them life like a present, all wrapped in white with every promise of happiness . . ."

THE DARK AT THE TOP OF THE STAIRS

"The von Trapp children don't play. They march."

THE SOUND OF MUSIC

"There won't ever be the patter of little feet in my house—unless I was to rent some mice."

PETE KELLY'S BLUES

"I am going to turn this kid into a decent, God-fearing Christian if I have to break every bone in his body."

AUNTIE MAME

"When middle-class sixteen-year-olds come up and ask for a hand-out, that's pathetic!"

THE CANDIDATE

"What will you give me for a basket of kisses?"
"A basket of hugs."

THE BAD SEED

"I don't understand these modern girls . . . Polly, for instance, sometimes she won't let you kiss her at all. But, there's Cynthia. She'll let you kiss her whenever you want . . ."

LOVE FINDS ANDY HARDY

"Pity he had no children."
"Oh, but I have. Thousands of them. And all boys."

GOODBYE, MR. CHIPS

"It spite of everything, I still believe that people are really good at heart."

THE DIARY OF ANNE FRANK

"Just because every child can't get its wish, that doesn't mean there isn't a Santa Claus."

MIRACLE ON 34TH STREET

"I refuse to endanger the health of my children in a house with less than three bathrooms."

MR. BLANDINGS BUILDS HIS DREAM HOUSE

"God bless Captain Vere!"

BILLY BUDD

"I wasn't popular at school on account of having no personality and not being pretty."

BADLANDS

"I can't believe I gave my panties to a geek."

SIXTEEN CANDLES

"A boy's best friend is his mother."

PSYCHO

"You would actually call our soon-to-be-conceived offspring Bozo?"

"Only if he's a boy."

LOVE STORY

"I wonder how a mother could call a boy Florenz."

FUNNY GIRL

"I made a deal with him when he was six . . . that he could use whatever name he wished, for however long he wished until his thirteenth birthday. . . . He went through a long period of dogs' names when he was little, King and Rover having a real vogue for awhile. For three months he referred to himself as Big Sam, then there was Little Max, Snoopy, Chip, Rocky, Rex, Mike, Martin, Lamont, Chevrolet, Woodrow, Lefty, The Phantom. He received his library card in the name of Rafael Sabatini . . ."

A THOUSAND CLOWNS

"I started at Amherst and I worked my way through the alphabet to Yale. I'm stuck there."

BUTTERFIELD 8

"Stay close to the young, and a little rubs off."

GIGI

"I had a very young week last week. It's not worth it."

A STAR IS BORN

"You're trying to run the school like a factory for turning out money-mad, machine-made snobs . . . Modern methods! Poppycock! Give a boy a sense of humor and a sense of promotion and he'll stand up to anything."

GOODBYE, MR. CHIPS

"It's a bit odd becoming a school girl at your age."

"Listen, you think it's easy being the only one in the class with clear skin?"

SAME TIME, NEXT YEAR

"Any man who hates children can't be all bad."

NEVER GIVE A SUCKER AN EVEN BREAK

"I'm a kid."
"Who isn't?"

BIG

"You brought music back into the house. I'd forgotten."

THE SOUND OF MUSIC

"Why, a four-year-old child can understand this report. Run out and find me a four-year-old child."

DUCK SOUP

"The happiest days are when babies come."

GONE WITH THE WIND

"Hey, I'm depraved on accounta I'm deprived."

WEST SIDE STORY

CHAPTER
NINETEEN

★

Sports

W hat are the sports that have most preoccupied the movies? Boxing has held a primal appeal, perhaps because of its violence and the ease with which the ring becomes a metaphor for life. The "Rocky" films, "Raging Bull," "Golden Boy," and "Body and Soul" are only a few of the films that have focused on fisticuffs. Pool has also attracted filmmakers, with movies like "The Hustler" and its sequel, "The Color of Money." Baseball has attracted its share of attention, with "Bull Durham," "Field of Dreams," "The Natural," and "Pride of the Yankees." Football appeared in "Semi-Tough," "Saturday's Hero," and "Heaven Can Wait," and horse racing was an element of films that ran the gamut from "A Day at the Races" to "My Fair Lady." Perhaps because the poetry of sports is mostly on the field, it has not exactly overflowed into the dialogue. Of course, Marlon Brando tells his brother, "I coulda been a contender" and a phantom tells Kevin Costner, "If you build it, he will come." And, of course, some of the wittiest comments ever to come out of a screenplay appear in the film "Bull Durham."

"If you build it, he will come."

FIELD OF DREAMS

"Fast Eddie, let's play some pool."

THE HUSTLER

"There's never been a ballplayer slept with me who didn't have the best year of his career."

BULL DURHAM

"I coulda had class . . . I coulda been somebody. Instead of a bum which is what I am."

ON THE WATERFRONT

"One dollar and you'll remember me all your life."
"That's the most nauseating proposition I've ever heard."

A DAY AT THE RACES

"Even if you beat me, I'm still the best."

THE HUSTLER

"I'd never sleep with a player hittin' under two hundred unless he had a lot of RBI's and was a great glove man up the middle."

BULL DURHAM

"Makin' love is like hittin' a baseball. You just gotta relax and concentrate."

BULL DURHAM

"I loved baseball since Arnold Rothstein fixed the world series in 1919."

GODFATHER II

"You're a loser 'cause you're dead inside."

THE HUSTLER

"Do you have anything light [to read]?"
"How about this leaflet, 'Famous Jewish Sports Legends'?"

AIRPLANE

"I love a little macho male bonding, even if it probably is latent homosexuality being rechanneled."

BULL DURHAM

"I consider myself the luckiest man on the face of the earth."

PRIDE OF THE YANKEES

"There can only be one winner, folks, but isn't that the American way?"

THEY SHOOT HORSES, DON'T THEY?

"Do you think Dwight Gooden leaves his socks on?"

BULL DURHAM

"From here on in, I rag nobody."

BANG THE DRUM SLOWLY

"You ever heard about Walt Whitman?"
"Who's he play for?"

BULL DURHAM

"Move your bloomin' ass!"

MY FAIR LADY

"[Boxing] is like any other business, only the blood shows."

CHAMPION

"[Boxing] is the only sport in the world where two guys get paid for doing something they'd be arrested for if they got drunk and did it for nothing."

CHAMPION

"Did I say killer? I meant champion. I get my boxing terms mixed."

ALL ABOUT EVE

"Fat man, you shoot a great game of pool."
"So do you, Fast Eddie."

THE HUSTLER

"I believe in the soul, the small of a woman's back, the hanging curve ball, high fiber, good scotch, long foreplay, show tunes . . . I believe that Lee Harvey

Oswald acted alone, I believe that there oughtta be a constitutional amendment outlawing astro-turf . . . I believe in the "sweet spot," voting every election, soft core pornography, chocolate chip cookies . . . and I believe in long, slow, deep, soft, wet kisses that last for three days."

BULL DURHAM

"A golf course is nothing but a poolroom moved outdoors."

GOING MY WAY

"Some day, when things are tough, maybe you can ask the boys to go in there and win just one for the gipper."

KNUTE ROCKNE—ALL AMERICAN

"When I die, in the newspapers they'll write that the sons-of-bitches of this world have lost their leader."

BANG THE DRUM SLOWLY

"Was it the Rose Bowl he made his famous run?"
"It was the punch bowl, honey."

CAT ON A HOT TIN ROOF

"What I give them lasts a lifetime, what they give me lasts a hundred forty-two games. Sometimes it seems a bad trade, but bad trades are part of baseball."

BULL DURHAM

"One long-ball hitter. That's what we need. I'd sell my soul for one long-ball hitter—hey, where did you come from?"

DAMN YANKEES

"Einstein couldn't kick a football across the dance floor, but he changed the shape of the universe."

A LETTER TO THREE WIVES

"Water polo? Isn't that terribly dangerous?"
"I'll say. I had two ponies drown under me."

SOME LIKE IT HOT

"Hey, is this heaven?"
"No, it's Iowa."

FIELD OF DREAMS

"Go for it."

ROCKY

CHAPTER
TWENTY

★

Death

Some very profound things have been said of death by the writers of "All Quiet on the Western Front," "Death Takes a Holiday," "Zorba the Greek," and "A Guy Named Joe." But the most memorable lines on the subject of death seem to be those of Woody Allen in "Love and Death" and "Hannah and Her Sisters." (It was Woody Allen who said, "I'm not afraid of dying, I just don't want to be there when it happens.") His quotes are memorable because they play off the usual portentousness that authors bring to the subject of death. Hollywood screenwriters, enjoying the pleasures of affluence and climate, seem to have less to say about death than about life. A classic case of denial. Sometimes, of course, screenwriters are all too aware of death and "old age—the only disease that you don't look forward to being cured of," as Herman Mankiewicz and Orson Welles wrote in "Citizen Kane." Samuel Goldwyn once upbraided Dorothy Parker for her distaste for happy endings in her scripts. Said Parker: "Mr. Goldwyn, there have been two billion life stories and not one of them ever had a happy ending."

"The key is to not think of death as an end but think of it more as a very effective way of cutting down on your expenses."

LOVE AND DEATH

"No man is really dead unless he breaks faith with the future. No man is really alive unless he accepts his responsibilities to it."

A GUY NAMED JOE

"Give me a little peace."
"A little? Why so modest? I'll give you *eternal* peace."

THE LION IN WINTER

"Have you ever talked to a corpse? It's boring."

AN AMERICAN WEREWOLF IN LONDON

"Would you care for a blindfold or an after-dinner mint?"

BLAZING SADDLES
to man about to be executed

"If history has taught us anything, it's that you can kill anybody."

THE GODFATHER

"I shall walk through the valley of death . . . in fact, now that I think of it, I shall *run* through the valley of death . . ."

LOVE AND DEATH

"Oh God, I'm so stupid. . . . Somehow I thought when she finally went that it would be a relief."

TERMS OF ENDEARMENT

"Don't be afraid, Carlo. Come on, you think I'd make my sister a widow?"

THE GODFATHER

"One moment, please—I'll connect you with heaven."

THREE COMRADES

"Hold it. Next man makes a move, the nigger gets it."

BLAZING SADDLES

black man holding gun
to his own head

"What makes you think you can get away with this? What are you going to do? Kill me? Everybody dies."

BODY AND SOUL

"In the end we will win. . . . As for those beneath the wooden crosses, we can only murmur thanks, pal, thanks."

THE STORY OF G.I. JOE

"I always tell people to hope for the best and prepare for the worst."
"And they let you get away with that?"

TERMS OF ENDEARMENT

"You sag, Renault, like an old woman . . . you're a corpse . . . go get yourself buried."

DINNER AT EIGHT

"That you, Martha? . . . I don't want to be disturbed."

DARK VICTORY

dying words to her maid

"There are worse things in life than death. I mean, if you've ever spent an evening with an insurance salesman . . ."

LOVE AND DEATH

"Death ends a life, but it does not end a relationship. . . ."

I NEVER SANG FOR MY FATHER

"All of a sudden, it's closer to the end than it is to the beginning, and death is suddenly a perceptible thing for me—with definite features."

NETWORK

"Maybe it's easy for the dying to be honest. I'm sick of you. I'm sick of your brothers and their dirty tricks to

make a dime. . . . You'll wreck this town, you and
your brothers. You'll wreck this country.''

THE LITTLE FOXES

"Every morning you come in yelling, 'Rise and shine!
Rise and shine!' I think, 'How lucky dead people
are.' ''

THE GLASS MENAGERIE

"You only gave me books with the word *death* in the
title.''

ANNIE HALL

"From all I've heard about heaven, it seems to be a
pretty unbusinesslike place. They could probably use a
good man like me.''

LIFE WITH FATHER

"When it comes to dying for your country, it's better
not to die at all.''

ALL QUIET ON THE WESTERN FRONT

"There is nothing wrong with suffering—if you suffer
for a purpose. Our revolution didn't abolish danger or
death. It simply made danger and death worthwhile.''

THINGS TO COME

"Then last week, as it must to all men, death came to
Charles Foster Kane.''

CITIZEN KANE

"Such a pretty name for a disease. Sounds like a rare
flower, doesn't it? Late-blooming dementia praecox.''

SUDDENLY LAST SUMMER

"Go on, Owen. Tell her I'm dying—and don't
overact.''

TWENTIETH CENTURY

"How old do you think I am?''
"Somewhere between forty and death.''

MAME

"Sometimes a dead man can be a terrible enemy."

VIVA ZAPATA!

"What can you say about a twenty-five-year-old girl who died? That she was beautiful. And brilliant. That she loved Mozart and Bach. And the Beatles. And me."

LOVE STORY

"The guy who kills me, I hope he does it because he hates my guts—not because it's his job."

DOG DAY AFTERNOON

"Just old age. It's the only disease . . . that you don't look forward to being cured of."

CITIZEN KANE

"Considering I've been dead for sixteen years, I'm in remarkable health."

BORN YESTERDAY

"It's quite possible, Octavian, that when you die, you will die without ever having been alive."

CLEOPATRA

"Oh, by the way, how was my funeral?"

MY FAVORITE WIFE

"I always look well when I'm near death."

CAMILLE

"Living, I'm worth nothing to her. But dead, I can buy her the tallest cathedrals. . . . One well-directed bullet will accomplish all that."

THE PETRIFIED FOREST

"I feel like we've died and gone to heaven—only we had to climb up."

BAREFOOT IN THE PARK

"Man is not made for defeat. Man can be destroyed but not defeated."

THE OLD MAN AND THE SEA

"I wish I had been born a man . . . the concerns are so simple: money and death."

A DELICATE BALANCE

"There are only two perfectly good men—one dead, the other unborn."

KLONDIKE ANNIE

"If anything happens to me, tell every woman I've ever gone out with I was talking about her at the end. That way they'll have to reevaluate me."

BROADCAST NEWS

"My Uncle Phil dropped dead playing squash. . . . The doctor suggested it for his health."

HANNAH AND HER SISTERS

"Listen to that bitch—the sea—that maker of widows."

ZORBA THE GREEK

"I was suicidal . . . and would have killed myself, but I was in analysis with a strict Freudian, and if you kill yourself, they make you pay for the sessions you miss."

ANNIE HALL

"All right! I shall kill myself!"
"Aw, don't minimize this."

THE TEAHOUSE OF THE AUGUST MOON

"You see, George, you've really had a wonderful life. Don't you see what a mistake it would be to throw it away?"

IT'S A WONDERFUL LIFE

"Where are you going?"
"To the river."
"What for?"
"To make a hole in it."

PYGMALION

"I had a good friend in the CIA had a stutter. Cost him his life, dammit."

A FISH CALLED WANDA

"Life is trouble. Only death is not. To be alive is to undo your belt and look for trouble."

ZORBA THE GREEK

"The first thing to do is to make sure that he's dead. I don't trust him."

WE'RE NO ANGELS

"I'll buy a gun and kill myself. . . . that would shatter my parents . . . I would have to kill them too. To spare them the grief."

HANNAH AND HER SISTERS

"Now, that was impertinent of him—to die with his rent unpaid."

A TALE OF TWO CITIES

"Dying is easy—comedy is hard."

MY FAVORITE YEAR

"I've been dead once already. It's very liberating."

BATMAN

"With all my heart, I still love the man I killed."

THE LETTER

"I have no fear of the gallows."
"No?"
"No. Why should I? They're gonna shoot me."

LOVE AND DEATH

"Catholicism for me was die now, pay later."

HANNAH AND HER SISTERS

"I already know a great many people. Until one of them dies I couldn't possibly meet anyone else."

CHARADE

CHAPTER
TWENTY-ONE

★

Miscellany

It is hard to say what makes any great motion picture great. Is it the special depth of the acting? Is it the subtle touch of the direction? Whatever the strange alchemy that makes a film memorable, arguably the most important ingredient is the words. This compendium is intended to return the attention of moviegoers to an appreciation of the words, the wit, the epigrams, the profundities, the wisecracks that help a movie make its points, get its laughs, create its characters, build its climaxes, and draw us into the wonderful communal and personal activity that we call "going to the movies."

"I'm willing to start at the bottom."
"You're aiming too high."

COCKTAIL

"We're Americans, with a capital *A*. Do you know what that means? It means that our forebears were kicked out of every decent country in the world."

STRIPES

"How about tomorrow night?"
"You know I can't plan that far in advance."

MIKE'S MURDER

"I was the intellectual equivalent of a ninety-eight pound weakling. I would go to the beach and people would kick copies of Byron in my face."

DEAD POETS SOCIETY

"I think this is the beginning of a beautiful friendship."

CASABLANCA

"Stingo, you look nice in your cocksucker suit."

SOPHIE'S CHOICE

"To me nature is spiders and bugs. And big fish eating little fish, and plants eating plants. It's like an enormous restaurant."

LOVE AND DEATH

"Look at the man with scars over his face."
"Let's find the man who gave him that face."

THE MAGNIFICENT SEVEN

"At this moment it's difficult to believe that you're so proud."
"At this moment it's difficult to believe that you're so prejudiced."

PRIDE AND PREJUDICE

"I just went gay, all of a sudden."

I WAS A MALE WAR BRIDE

"The ark is something that man was not meant to disturb . . . It's a radio for speaking to God."

RAIDERS OF THE LOST ARK

"There's a lot of money in tear gas."

THE HEARTBREAK KID

"No wire hangers!"

MOMMIE DEAREST

"I long for serenity, security, and all that jazz."

KITTEN WITH A WHIP

"Yes, I heard you, I heard you. A deaf man could hear you!"

HISTORY OF THE WORLD—PART I
Moses to the Lord

"I don't know why we're out of aspirin. I thought we ordered the family size."

WILL SUCCESS SPOIL ROCK HUNTER?

"I'm comparatively normal for a man who grew up in Brooklyn."

ANNIE HALL

"When the toucan cries, danger is not far."

THE EMERALD FOREST

"At the sound of the falling tree, it's nine-thirty."

BLUE VELVET

"The first time I put that polka-dot dress in the washing machine, it fell all to pieces. Those little polka dots just dropped right off in the water."

CRIMES OF THE HEART

"Why, you're just as perfectly sane as anyone walking the streets of Hazelhurst, Mississippi."

CRIMES OF THE HEART

"You'll be a Presbyterian, Roger, isn't that nice?"

CARBON COPY

"You don't want to play the game as a white man, so they're going to let you watch it as a black man."

CARBON COPY

"I read *Gone With the Wind* twice a year."

RICH AND FAMOUS

"Only in Times Square the dawn gets turned on by an electrician."

GUYS AND DOLLS

"Don't fuck with me, fellas. I've fought bigger sharks than you."

MOMMIE DEAREST

"I tried to sell out to you but I couldn't close the deal."

COCKTAIL

"[This place is] a proctologist's dream. Assholes wall to wall."

COCKTAIL

"Will you check about the hors d'oeuvres? The caterer forgot them, the varnish wasn't dry . . ."

ALL ABOUT EVE

"I'm sure he's into some heavy ideas. Like primal screaming."

ANNIE HALL

"It is a lovely day . . . which would indicate that the night is over."

ARTHUR

"My whole family's been having nothing but trouble with immigrants since they came to this country."

FINIAN'S RAINBOW

"Let's play the truth game."

THE BOYS IN THE BAND

"He takes to the street and for a while he earns a meager living selling meagers."

TAKE THE MONEY AND RUN

"We couldn't admire him when we weren't allowed to read him, could we?"

DOCTOR ZHIVAGO

"It is my understanding that the Constitution of the United States allows everybody their free choice between cheesecake and strudel."

GUYS AND DOLLS

"Mama, that's the first time I stopped hugging first. I like that."

TERMS OF ENDEARMENT

"No cigarettes either? . . . Don't you miss the coughing and the hacking in the morning?"

CALIFORNIA SUITE

"I like being famous. You know what happens when I go shopping for groceries now? I'm famous. I buy mayonnaise and I'm famous."

JULIA

"Things are hopeless . . . but they're not serious."

FINIAN'S RAINBOW

"I am not a father figure. I am not an uncle figure or a brother or a cousin figure. In fact, the only figure I intend being is a total stranger figure."

FATHER GOOSE

"Guess who's coming to dinner."

GUESS WHO'S COMING TO DINNER

"Here is my hope that Robert Conway will find his Shangri-La."

"Here is my hope that we all find our Shangri-La."

LOST HORIZON

"May I have this dance, Mother?"

TO EACH HIS OWN

"I'm tired of playing second fiddle to the ghost of Beethoven."

HUMORESQUE

"With Major Lawrence, mercy is a passion. With me, it is merely good manners. You may judge which motive is more reliable."

LAWRENCE OF ARABIA

"If you come back to me, I shall treat you just as I have always treated you. I can't change my nature, and I don't intend to change my manners."

MY FAIR LADY

"The man of the house has got to have a pair of boots because he's got to do a lot of kicking."

PICNIC

"I am sitting here . . . toying with the idea of removing your heart and stuffing it—like an olive."

NOTHING SACRED

"Too bad it didn't happen further down the street—in front of the May Company. From them you can collect. Couldn't you have dragged yourself another twenty feet?"

THE FORTUNE COOKIE
lawyer to an injured client

"I got brown sandwiches and green sandwiches . . . it's either very new cheese or very old meat."

THE ODD COUPLE

"I always get the fuzzy end of the lollipop."

SOME LIKE IT HOT

"He just swallowed his pride. It'll take him a moment or two to digest it."

THE HASTY HEART

"This proves that the U.S. Government recognizes this man, Kris Kringle, to be the one and only Santa Claus."

MIRACLE ON 34TH STREET

"Fred C. Dobbs don't say nuthin' he don't mean."

THE TREASURE OF THE SIERRA MADRE

"Now when the Reverend Mr. Playfair, good man that he is, comes down, I wants yez all to cheer like Protestants."

THE QUIET MAN

"These days, a man doesn't know whether he's driving a car or an animal. Mustangs. Jaguars. Pintos."

HARRY AND TONTO

"Martha, will you show her where we keep the euphemism?"

WHO'S AFRAID OF VIRGINIA WOOLF?

"When I get through with you, you'll look like—well what do you call beautiful? A tree? You'll look like a tree."

FUNNY FACE

"I believe in Rhett Butler. He's the only cause I know. The rest doesn't mean much to me."

GONE WITH THE WIND

"I believe in the human heart now only as a doctor."

LOVE IS A MANY-SPLENDORED THING

"I believe I am past my prime. I had reckoned on my prime lasting till I was at least fifty."

THE PRIME OF MISS JEAN BRODIE

"I don't know nothin' about birthin' babies."

GONE WITH THE WIND

"Irving R. Feldman's birthday is my own personal national holiday . . . He is proprietor of perhaps the most distinguished kosher delicatessen in our neighborhood . . ."

A THOUSAND CLOWNS

"My blood *circulates*. I'm not saying everywhere, but it circulates."

THE SUNSHINE BOYS

"Your body! After all, what is it? Just a physical covering, that's all—worth chemically thirty-two cents."

HERE COMES MR. JORDAN

"I want to look somebody up. Does this office have a copy of 'Who's Still Who'?"

SILK STOCKINGS

"I'm afraid of nothing, except being bored."

CAMILLE

"Jonathan is more than a man. He's an experience—
and he's habit-forming. If they could ever bottle him,
he'd outsell ginger ale."

THE BAD AND THE BEAUTIFUL

"You can't show your bosom 'fore three o'clock."

GONE WITH THE WIND

"Now you've done it! Now you have done it! . . . .
You tore off one of my chests."

SOME LIKE IT HOT

"They have given you a new title, Divinity:
Incendiary."

QUO VADIS

"They say he ain't scared of nothing. If he wants the
picture of a lion, he just goes up to him and says,
'Look pleasant.' "

KING KONG

"I don't go to church. Kneeling bags my nylons."

THE BIG CARNIVAL

"I am married to an American agent."

NOTORIOUS

"What do you got in place of a conscience? Don't
answer. I know—a lawyer."

DETECTIVE STORY

"The Gospel according to Brady! God speaks to Brady,
and Brady tells the world!"

INHERIT THE WIND

"Miss Kubelik, one doesn't get to be a second
administrative assistant around here unless he's a pretty
good judge of character . . ."

THE APARTMENT

"Don't drop into the chair. *Insinuate* yourself."

GIGI

"A salesman's got to dream, boy. It comes with the territory."

DEATH OF A SALESMAN

"I suspect a plot. This fish looks blue to me. Very blue. In fact, it looks despondent."

AH, WILDERNESS!

"Mr. Kane was a man who got everything he wanted, and then lost it. Maybe Rosebud was something he couldn't get or something he lost."

CITIZEN KANE

"Burn a city in order to create an epic? That's carrying the principle of art for art's sake too far."

QUO VADIS

"I'm not one of those eye-for-an-eye men. I always take two eyes."

WAKE OF THE RED WITCH

"That color looks wonderful with your eyes."
"Just the right eye. I hate what it does to the left."

FUNNY GIRL

"I think it would be fun to run a newspaper."

CITIZEN KANE

"Getting a clear picture on channel two is not my idea of whoopee."

THE ODD COUPLE

"The only fun I get is feeding the goldfish, and they only eat once a day."

BORDERTOWN

"I'm a good girl, I am."

PYGMALION

"Good morning, Mr. Beale. They tell me you're a madman."

NETWORK

"To raise one hundred dollars, I would have to sell thirteen thousand hamburgers between now and six . . . Do you know anybody that's that hungry?"

THE MATING SEASON

"We can spend the whole day doing things we've never done before. We'll take turns—first something you've never done, then me—of course, I can't really think of anything I've never done."

BREAKFAST AT TIFFANY'S

"If I don't come back with the biggest story you ever handled, you can put me back in short pants and make me marble editor."

NOTHING SACRED

"Doctor, I'm going to tell you something I've never told anyone before . . . sometimes I see that big rabbit myself."

HARVEY

"It's just my imagination. Some people have flat feet. Some people have dandruff. I have this appalling imagination."

THE SEVEN YEAR ITCH

"I did just what she told me. I lived! I've got to find out what to do now."

AUNTIE MAME

"You make out like every young girl was Jennifer Jones in 'The Song of Bernadette.' "

COME BACK, LITTLE SHEBA

"When will you learn that I am *always* kind and courteous! Bring the idiot in."

THE MAN WHO CAME TO DINNER

"We were above that in Covent Garden . . . I sold flowers. I didn't sell myself. Now you've made a lady of me, I'm not fit to sell anything else."

PYGMALION

"Where the devil are my slippers, Eliza?"

Pygmalion

'Campers! The Entertainment Committee was quite disappointed in the really poor turnout at this morning's community sing.''

A Thousand Clowns

'I can't stand a naked light bulb any more than I can stand a rude remark or a vulgar action.''

A Streetcar Named Desire

'There are some times a man has to fight his way through.''

'Wouldn't it be better to think your way through?''

The Bells of St. Mary's

"I'm sorry. I don't like people touching my blue blanket.''

The Producers

'It seemed like a good idea at the time.''

The Last Flight

'We have one simple rule here—be kind.''

Lost Horizon

'He has a heart of gold—only harder.''

A Star Is Born

'Mad? Mad? Hannibal was mad, Caesar was mad, and Napoleon was surely maddest of them all.''

Gunga Din

'Pay no attention to the man behind the curtain . . . the . . . er . . . Great Oz has spoken.''

The Wizard of Oz

'I guess Rosebud is just a piece in a jigsaw puzzle . . . a missing piece.''

Citizen Kane

'I stick my neck out for nobody.''

Casablanca

"It has occurred to us that, if there should be several pair of young male elephants turned loose in forest of America, we are of opinion that, after a while, they will increase in number."

THE KING AND I
the king dictating a letter to President Lincoln

"Frederic, you must stop this Polinaise jangle."

A SONG TO REMEMBER

"I hate the dawn. The grass always looks as though it's been left out all night."

THE DARK CORNER

"King Solomon had the right idea about work. 'Whatever thy hand findeth to do,' Solomon said, 'do thy doggonedest.' "

LIFE WITH FATHER

"I've wrestled with reality for thirty-five years, and I'm happy, Doctor. I finally won out over it."

HARVEY

"Just head for that big star straight on. The highway's under it, and it'll take us right home."

THE MISFIT

"You dare to dicker with your Pontiff?"

THE AGONY AND THE ECSTASY

"What's the going price on integrity this week?"

I'LL NEVER FORGET WHAT'S 'IS NAME

"I cannot stand little notes on my pillow. 'We are out of corn flakes. F.U.' It took me three hours to figure out F.U. was Felix Unger."

THE ODD COUPLE

"Now all you have to do is hold the chicken, bring me the toast, [and] give me a check for the chicken salad sandwich. . . ."

FIVE EASY PIECES

"I hate the beach. I hate the sun. I'm pale and I'm redheaded. I don't tan—I stroke."

PLAY IT AGAIN, SAM

"Willkommen, bienvenue, welcome."

CABARET

"Some day a real man will come and wash this scum off the street."

TAXI DRIVER

"I made the seeds too big."

OH, GOD!
God considering avocados

"How would you like to stand around dressed like a head waiter for the last seven hundred years?"

LOVE AT FIRST BITE

"There's nothing more inconvenient than an old queen with a head cold."

VICTOR/VICTORIA

"My name is Inigo Montoya. You killed my father—prepare to die."

THE PRINCESS BRIDE

"I got the tides to regulate. I got no time for flatulence and orgasms."

THE ADVENTURES OF BARON MUNCHAUSEN

"I don't mind if you don't like my manners. I don't like 'em myself . . . I grieve over them long winter evenings."

THE BIG SLEEP

"You're my father, I'm your son. I love you . . . but you think of yourself as a colored man. I think of myself as a man."

GUESS WHO'S COMING TO DINNER

"When I'm standing up, my mind's lying down. When I'm lying down, my mind's standing . . ."

YOUNG MR. LINCOLN

"We had some money put aside for a rainy day, but we didn't know it was going to get this wet."

MAME

"What a story! Everything but the bloodhounds snapping at her rear end."

ALL ABOUT EVE

"For me, a little German music goes a long way."

SHIP OF FOOLS

"Physical Ed? Who's he?"

PAT AND MIKE

"In my case, self-absorption is completely justified. I have never discovered any other subject quite so worthy of my attention."

LAURA

"You know what's wrong with New Mexico? . . . Too much outdoors. Give me those eight spindly trees in front of Rockefeller Center any day."

ACE IN THE HOLE

"I never did like the idea of sitting on a newspaper. I did it once, and all the headlines came off on my white pants . . . Nobody bought a paper that day. They just followed me around all over town and read the news on the seat of my pants."

IT HAPPENED ONE NIGHT

"I think I'll have a large order of 'prognosis negative.' "

DARK VICTORY

"Close your eyes and tap your heels together three times. And think to yourself, 'There's no place like home.' "

THE WIZARD OF OZ

"Wuz you ever bit by a dead bee?"

TO HAVE AND HAVE NOT

"I have nothing to apologize for. I take pride. I am the best possible Arnold Burns."

A THOUSAND CLOWNS

"I'm more interested in the Rock of Ages than I am in the age of rocks."

INHERIT THE WIND

"People here are funny. They work so hard at living they forget how to live."

MR. DEEDS GOES TO TOWN

"You think you're not in prison now, living in a gray little room, going to a gray little job, leading a gray little life?"

THE PRODUCERS

"I'm what is known as a paid companion."
"I didn't know that companionship could be bought."

REBECCA

"Simple phonetics . . . I can place a man within six miles. I can place him within two miles in London. Sometimes within two blocks."

MY FAIR LADY

"There was a land of cavaliers and cotton fields called the Old South . . . Look for it only in books, for it is no more than a dream remembered, a civilization gone with the wind."

GONE WITH THE WIND

"For those who believe in God, no explanation is necessary. For those who do not believe in God, no explanation is possible."

THE SONG OF BERNADETTE

"I should have hastened to my psychiatrist. He told me never to trust anyone but him."

PILLOW TALK

"At fifty dollars an hour, all my cases interest me."

THE SEVEN YEAR ITCH

"I hope you die soon. I'm waiting for you to die."

THE LITTLE FOXES

"I can't get with any religion that advertises in *Popular Mechanics*."

ANNIE HALL

"Rome is an eternal thought in the mind of God."

SPARTACUS

"It's detestable, but that's the way it is. It's even worse in New Canaan. There, nobody can sell or rent to a Jew . . . There's sort of a gentlemen's agreement . . ."

GENTLEMEN'S AGREEMENT

"If you've got anything on your chest besides your chin, you'd better get it off."

THE ODD COUPLE

"This is your neighbor speaking. I'm sure I speak for all of us when I say that something must be done about your garbage cans in the alley here. *It is definitely second-rate garbage!*"

A THOUSAND CLOWNS

"I'd punch you right in the nose if I wasn't afraid you'd break my jaw."

THE BACHELOR AND THE BOBBY-SOXER

"Your eyes are full of hate, forty-one. That's good. Hate keeps a man alive. It gives him strength."

BEN-HUR

"We're not quarreling. We're in complete agreement. We hate each other."

THE BAND WAGON

"I can't afford to hate anybody. I'm only a photographer."

THE PHILADELPHIA STORY

"They created a lot of grand palaces here. But they forgot about the noblemen to put in them."

MR. DEEDS GOES TO TOWN

"This is for ladies only!"

"So is this, madam. But every now and again I have to run some water through it."

MY FAVORITE YEAR
man using a ladies' room

"I do hateful things for which people love me, and I do lovable things for which people hate me."

INHERIT THE WIND

"That's wonderful, sir, wonderful. I do like a man who tells me right out that he's looking out for himself. Don't we all? I don't trust a man who says he's not."

THE MALTESE FALCON

"You know, since I started taking Lithium, I feel more sensible than this month's *Good Housekeeping*."

AN UNMARRIED WOMAN

"Well, if you look at it, it's a barn. If you smell it, it's a stable."

MONKEY BUSINESS

"Grand Hotel. Always the same. People come. People go. Nothing ever happens."

GRAND HOTEL

"Just listen to this stomach of mine. Way it sounds, you'd think I had a hyena inside me."

THE AFRICAN QUEEN

"Every day, up at the crack of noon."

MAME

"Oh, hello there. Is this Mary Feeney?. . . . This is Marty Pilletti. I wonder if you recall me . . ."

MARTY

"Hello—is this someone with good news or money? No? Good-bye."

A THOUSAND CLOWNS
answering phone

"Well, my little pretty, I can cause accidents, too."

THE WIZARD OF OZ

"My check-out time in any hotel in the world is when I check out."

SWEET BIRD OF YOUTH

"He pulled a knife on me. A kitchen knife. It was still dirty from breakfast."

THE SUNSHINE BOYS

"When you're slapped, you'll take it and like it."

THE MALTESE FALCON

"I'm sorry, sir. I could never answer to a whistle. Whistles are for dogs or cats and other animals but not for children and definitely not for me."

THE SOUND OF MUSIC

"Oh, brilliant, merciful master, let me out and I will grant you three wishes."

THE THIEF OF BAGDAD

"You've got your wish: you've never been born."

IT'S A WONDERFUL LIFE

"I have no scepter, but I have a pen."

VOLTAIRE

"I don't use a pen. I write with a goose quill dipped in venom."

LAURA

"This guy walks into a psychiatrist's office with a duck on his head. Psychiatrist says, 'Can I help you?' The duck says, 'Yeah, get this guy off my ass.' "

MY FAVORITE YEAR

"I get pregnant if we drink from the same cup."

SAME TIME, NEXT YEAR

"I don't think this engine can get very far on dry martinis."

MURDER BY DEATH

"Who's going to believe you're sixty-four?"
"Sixty-three-year-old ladies."

AFTER THE FOX

"I know I must look funny to you. Maybe if you came
to Mandrake Falls, you'd look just as funny to us . . .
but nobody'd laugh at you and make you ridiculous—
'cause that wouldn't be good manners."

MR. DEEDS GOES TO TOWN

"It's money and adventure and fame. It's the thrill of a
lifetime."

KING KONG

"Ladies are unwell . . . gentlemen vomit."

MY FAVORITE YEAR

"I know a lot of you are saying to yourself, 'He's
asking for a miracle.' . . . But I see it happen once a
year . . . at Christmas time."

MEET JOHN DOE

"In the southeast they say if you want to go to heaven
you have to change planes in Atlanta."

THE ACCIDENTAL TOURIST

"Don't listen to what your school teachers tell you . . .
Just see what they look like and that's how you'll know
what life is really going to be like."

CRIMES AND MISDEMEANORS

"I hear that *Commentary* and *Dissent* merged and
formed *Dysentery*."

ANNIE HALL

"I was in analysis for years. Nothing happened. My
poor analyst got so frustrated, the guy finally put in a
salad bar."

HANNAH AND HER SISTERS

"All right, so I'll go to the Stardust Ballroom. I'll put on my blue suit, and I'll go. And you know what I'm going to get for my trouble? Heartache."

MARTY

"Laugh now, Heathcliff. There's no laughter in hell."

WUTHERING HEIGHTS

"Where's the rest of me?"

KINGS ROW

"All of you know what I stand for—what I believe. I believe in the truth of the Book of Genesis. Exodus. Leviticus. Numbers. Deuteronomy. Joshua. Judges . . ."

INHERIT THE WIND

"We need a bigger boat."

JAWS

"I am not an animal!"

THE ELEPHANT MAN

"Th-th-that's all, folks."

WHAT'S UP, DOC?

CHAPTER
TWENTY-TWO
★
Censored Lines

The Hollywood censorship code laid down strict moral guidelines for the movies. The code created the infamous agency, the Hays Office. On hearing how much sex wound up on the cutting room floor, Fred Allen said, "It sounds uncomfortable, but that's Hollywood." Here are some of the lines that Mr. Hays and his staff deleted from screenplays as writers winced. They constitute an amusing anthology and are a fitting end to this collection as a warning against future repressions. To review these rather tame lines is to see just how puerile the censors were. They pressed Selznick to kill Rhett's closing line in "Gone With the Wind," saying: "David, there must be other ways Rhett Butler can express that thought. He could say, 'Frankly, Scarlett, it's a matter of indifference.' " The censors' rules seem innocent today, but they mirrored public standards: divorce was taboo, toilets and navels were invisible, and so on. As our views changed, the censors became obsolete. This led to an excess of sex and violence in the movies, which led to new threats of censorship, which led to today's self-censorship under the ratings system. Between the tendency of some to prohibit that which they disapprove, and the effort of some to exploit what

the traffic will bear, free expression remains an uncertain
freedom.

"Now madam, lie right down and tell me your troubles.
You needn't be afraid to talk to me—I used to be a
floorwalker in a ladies' washroom."

MONKEY BUSINESS

"I've known and admired your husband for years and
what's good enough for him is good enough for me."

MONKEY BUSINESS

"You have me at a disadvantage."
"Not yet."

MONKEY BUSINESS

"It used to take a villa in Cannes and a string of pearls.
Now all I ask is an exit visa."

CASABLANCA

"How extravagant you are, throwing away women like
that. Some day they may be rationed."

CASABLANCA

"That's Any-time Annie."

42ND STREET

"Afraid I gotta run."
"First door to your left."

42ND STREET

"She makes forty-five dollars a week and sends her
mother a hundred of it."

42ND STREET

"I'm getting the lay of the land."

THE FRENCH LINE

"She puts the *l* in lech . . ."

THE FRENCH LINE

"It was nice to have known you—three or four times."

PAL JOEY

"Two years, Vera, that's a long time between drinks."

PAL JOEY

"Why not? I've tried all the other rooms."

GUYS AND DOLLS
*when the desk clerk suggests
the bridal suite*

"Let it lie where you're softest."

DUEL IN THE SUN

"Love to him was nothin' more than what takes place
in the barn."

DUEL IN THE SUN

"Are you sure you have everything, Otis?"

"I haven't had any complaints yet."

A NIGHT AT THE OPERA
mounting gangplank

"Will you please get off the bed. What will people
say?"

"They'll probably say you're a very lucky woman."

A NIGHT AT THE OPERA

"Mrs. Claypool has decided to dispense with your
services."

"Why, she hasn't even had them yet."

A NIGHT AT THE OPERA

"Park your south end on the chair."

DOUBLE INDEMNITY

"Where they put me on the couch . . . when things
were done to me."

FOR WHOM THE BELL TOLLS

"This is just like bein' married, ain't it? It's better."

FROM HERE TO ETERNITY

"That girl blowed my fuse."

FROM HERE TO ETERNITY

"He's the illegitimate son of President Wilson."

A FAREWELL TO ARMS

"I used to think that when it happened I'd want to cry."

A FAREWELL TO ARMS

"This is our mirror room, very popular."

A FAREWELL TO ARMS

"My little white-breasted dove."

DR. JEKYLL AND MR. HYDE

"I made him, as they say, 'in God's own image.' "

THE BRIDE OF FRANKENSTEIN

"It's a waste of money training eunuchs."

SPARTACUS

"I've been lonely for you—night after night in my little room at the sanitarium—Room 412."

A DAY AT THE RACES

"No, Doctor, please don't go. I'll take care of your salary."
"Oh yeah? The last job I had, I had to take it out in trade, and this is no butcher shop. Not yet, anyhow."

A DAY AT THE RACES

"She told me things I could never repeat to a living soul . . ."

REBECCA

"What this party needs is a little gland treatment."

NOTORIOUS

"I think it would be wonderful to have a man love you so much he'd kill for you."

STRANGERS ON A TRAIN

"When General Motors has to go to the bathroom ten times a day, the whole country's ready to let go."

REAR WINDOW

"Today you can't tell a petting party from an Army physical."

REAR WINDOW

"This isn't any place for you. You're halfway decent. You don't know it but you're up to your knees in slime."

MR. SMITH GOES TO WASHINGTON

"Nuts!"

MR. DEEDS GOES TO TOWN

"My orders are to stick to your tail."

"I don't want anybody sticking to my tail."

MR. DEEDS GOES TO TOWN

"Oh, confound it, madam, if he wants the pants let him have them."

TOPPER

"We ain't burglars. We're hungry."

MODERN TIMES

"Take me to a culvert—I want to spew."

THE BANK DICK

"Take the castor oil for two nights running."

THE BANK DICK

"She looks like the Mona Lisa—only a little heavier."

THE BANK DICK

"I'm a one-man woman—one man at a time."

I'M NO ANGEL

"Make 'em wait for it."

I'M NO ANGEL

"It isn't the men in your life, it's the life in your men."

I'M NO ANGEL

"Men are at their best when women are at their worst."

KLONDIKE ANNIE

"Give a man a free hand and he puts it all over you."

KLONDIKE ANNIE

"When she is caught between two evils, she likes to take the one she never tried before."

KLONDIKE ANNIE

"If you don't act friendly, I don't act friendly, if you know what I mean."

BORN YESTERDAY

"Are you one of these talkers, or would you be innarested in a little action?"

BORN YESTERDAY

"Let me give you some advice, sonny boy. Never shovel it with a shoveler."

BORN YESTERDAY

"You have the touch of a sex-starved cobra."

THE MAN WHO CAME TO DINNER

"You could practically see the airport."

THE MAN WHO CAME TO DINNER
referring to filmy gown

"This brassiere was once worn by Hedy Lamarr."

THE MAN WHO CAME TO DINNER

"She is poised only to change girdles and check her oil."

THE MAN WHO CAME TO DINNER

"You damned impudent slut."

PYGMALION

"Of course [your intentions are honorable], Governor. If I thought they wasn't, I'd ask for fifty pounds."

PYGMALION

"The first night you came here, remember? You said I wouldn't have to worry. You said nothing would happen. Remember?"

A PLACE IN THE SUN

"What the hell's so special in bed?"

GOLDEN BOY

"A woman's place is in the hay."

GOLDEN BOY

"I'm a tramp from Newark, Tom, I know a dozen ways."

GOLDEN BOY

"Stop looking down her dress."

GOLDEN BOY

"Screw, Sweety."

WHO'S AFRAID OF VIRGINIA WOOLF?

"The sacrifice is usually a somewhat more private portion of the anatomy."

WHO'S AFRAID OF VIRGINIA WOOLF?

"You can't get an annulment if there's entrance."

WHO'S AFRAID OF VIRGINIA WOOLF?

"Protect your plow."

WHO'S AFRAID OF VIRGINIA WOOLF?

Epilogue

Chances are that like everyone else, you have your own favorite lines from your own favorite movies. It is the birthright of any American moviegoer. Some perfectly splendid lines, I dare say, have been omitted from this work. Sorry about that. But it is better to light a small candle than to curse the darkness. It is better to let me know the lines I've omitted than to curse the anthologist.

Write and tell me the lines I've overlooked and the movies they're from, so I can include them in a future edition of this work. I would like to offer a T-shirt bearing the words "I Coulda Been A Contender" to anyone whose lines are included in a future book. I really would like to do that. Unfortunately, no such T-shirts exist. Your reward will have to be the knowledge that the screenwriter who wrote the lines will have the satisfaction of seeing them preserved for posterity. He will experience the rush of pleasure that comes to creative people when they see that their work has struck a spark in the moviegoer's memory. That, plus the money, is what balances out the humiliations of the screenwriter's craft.

Parlor Game

A modest suggestion. "I Coulda Been A Contender" can form the basis for a dandy parlor game that you and your friends can enjoy. Monopoly and Trivial Pursuit don't rate at all when compared to the fun and gaiety of this one.

Simply recite a line from a movie and challenge your opponent to name the movie in which it appeared. My daughter tells me that she has spent many enjoyable evenings playing this game with friends as others protest, "Whose idea was this anyhow?" She finds it much more enjoyable than rolling dice and pushing little red hotels around a board. Extra points can be awarded for naming stars, studio, or director, and a special award can be presented to anyone who can name the screenwriter, who made it all happen.

APPENDIX

The following data applies to the films from which lines have been excerpted: Year of release, studio, screenwriter, author of work from which film was adapted, director, stars.

KEY TO ABBREVIATIONS OF PRODUCTION COMPANIES

AA	Allied Artists
AIP	American International
BV	Buena Vista
Col.	Columbia Pictures
MGM	Metro-Goldwyn-Mayer
Ori.	Orion Productions
Par.	Paramount Pictures
Rep.	Republic Pictures
RKO	RKO Radio Pictures
20th	Twentieth Century Fox Film Corporation
Tou.	Touchstone Productions, Buena Vista Releasing
Tri.	Tri-Star Pictures
UA	United Artists
Univ.	Universal Pictures, Universal-International

WB   Warner Brothers Pictures and First National Pictures

ABBOTT AND COSTELLO MEET FRANKEN-STEIN (1948) Univ. Original screenplay by Robert Lees, Frederic Renaldo, John Grant. Directed by Charles Barton. Starring Bud Abbott, Lou Costello, Lon Chaney, Bela Lugosi.

ACE IN THE HOLE (1951) Par. AKA THE BIG CARNIVAL. Screenplay by Billy Wilder, Lesser Samuels, Walter Newman. Directed by Billy Wilder. Starring Kirk Douglas, Jan Sterling, Peter Hall.

ACCIDENTAL TOURIST (1989) WB. Screenplay by Frank Galati and Lawrence Kasdan, from the novel by Anne Tyler. Directed by Lawrence Kasdan. Starring William Hurt, Kathleen Turner, Geena Davis.

ACROSS THE PACIFIC (1942) WB. Screenplay by Richard Macauley. Directed by John Huston. Starring Humphrey Bogart, Mary Astor, Sydney Greenstreet.

ADVENTURES OF BARON MUNCHAUSEN, THE (1990) Col. Screenplay by Charles McKeown and Terry Gilliam. Directed by Terry Gilliam. Starring John Neville and Robin Williams.

ADVENTURES OF BUCKAROO BANZAI, THE (1985) 20th. Screenplay by Earl MacRauch. Directed by W.D. Richter. Starring Peter Weller, John Lithgow, Ellen Barkin, Jeff Goldblum.

ADVENTURES OF MARK TWAIN, THE (1944) WB. Screenplay by Harold Sherman, Alan le May, Harry Chandler. Directed by Irving Rapper. Starring Fredric March, Alexis Smith, Donald Crisp.

ADVISE AND CONSENT (1962) Col. Screenplay by Wendell Mayes, from the novel by Allen Drury. Directed by Otto Preminger. Starring Henry Fonda, Walter Pidgeon, Charles Laughton, Don Murray, Franchot Tone.

AFFAIR TO REMEMBER, AN (1957) 20th. Written by Delmer Daves, Leo McCarey. Directed by Leo McCarey. Starring Cary Grant, Deborah Kerr.

AFRICAN QUEEN, THE (1951) UA. Screenplay by James Agee and John Huston. Based on the novel by C.S. Forester. Directed by John Huston. Starring Humphrey Bogart and Katharine Hepburn.

AGONY AND THE ECSTASY, THE (1965) 20th. Screenplay by Philip Dunne. Directed by Carol Reed. Starring Charlton Heston and Rex Harrison.

AH, WILDERNESS! (1935) MGM. Screenplay by Albert Hackett and Frances Goodrich, from the play by Eugene O'Neill. Directed by Clarence Brown. Starring Wallace Beery, Lionel Barrymore.

AIR FORCE (1943) WB. Screenplay by Dudley Nichols. Directed by Leo Forbstein. Starring John Garfield, Gig Young, Harry Carey.

AIRPLANE (1988) Par. Written and directed by Jim Abrahams, David and Jerry Zucker. Starring Robert Hays and Julie Haggerty.

ALFIE (1966) Par. Screenplay by Bill Naughton, based on his play. Directed by Lewis Gilbert. Starring Michael Caine, Shelley Winters, Millicent Martin.

ALGIERS (1938) Walter Wanger. Screenplay by Howard Lawson, James M. Cain. Directed by John Cromwell. Starring Charles Boyer and Hedy Lamarr.

ALICE DOESN'T LIVE HERE ANYMORE (1974) WB. Screenplay by Robert Getchell. Directed by Martin Scorsese. Starring Ellen Burstyn, Kris Kristofferson, Diane Ladd, Harvey Keitel.

ALIENS (1987) 20th. Screenplay and directed by

James Cameron. Starring Sigourney Weaver and Paul Reiser.

ALL ABOUT EVE (1950) 20th. Screenplay and directed by Joseph Mankiewicz. Starring Bette Davis, Anne Baxter, George Sanders, Celeste Holm.

ALL MY SONS (1948) Univ. Screenplay by Chester Erskine, from a play by Arthur Miller. Directed by Irving Reis. Starring Edward G. Robinson, Burt Lancaster.

ALL QUIET ON THE WESTERN FRONT (1930) Univ. Screenplay by Dell Andrews, Maxwell Anderson, and George Abbott. Based on the novel by Erich Maria Remarque. Directed by Lewis Milestone. Starring Lew Ayres, Louis Wolheim.

ALL THAT JAZZ (1979) 20th-Col. Screenplay by Robert Alan Arthur and Bob Fosse. Directed by Bob Fosse. Starring Roy Scheider, Jessica Lange, Cliff Gorman.

AMADEUS (1984) Screenplay by Peter Shaffer, from his play. Directed by Milos Forman. Starring F. Murray Abraham, Tom Hulce.

AMERICAN IN PARIS, AN (1951) MGM. Screenplay by Alan Jay Lerner. Directed by Vincente Minnelli. Starring Gene Kelly, Leslie Caron, Oscar Levant.

ANASTASIA (1956) 20th. Screenplay by Arthur Laurents, from the play by Marcella Maurette. Directed by Anatole Litvak. Starring Ingrid Bergman, Yul Brynner, Helen Hayes.

ANGELS WITH DIRTY FACES (1938) WB. Screenplay by John Westey and Warren Duff. Directed by Michael Curtiz. Starring James Cagney, Pat O'Brien, Humphrey Bogart, Ann Sheridan.

ANIMAL CRACKERS (1930) Par. Screenplay by Morrie Ryskind, Pierre Collings. Based on the musical by

George S. Kaufman, Morrie Ryskind, Harry Ruby, and Bert Kalmar. Directed by Victor Herman. Starring Groucho, Chico, and Harpo Marx, Margaret Dumont.

ANNA CHRISTIE (1930) MGM. Screenplay by Frances Marion. Based on the play by Eugene O'Neill. Directed by Charles Brown. Starring Greta Garbo, Charles Bickford.

ANNIE (1983) Col. Screenplay by Carol Sobieski. Based on the musical play by Thomas Meehan, and the cartoon strip created by Harold Gray. Directed by John Huston. Starring Aileen Quinn, Albert Finney, Carol Burnett.

ANNIE HALL (1977) UA. Screenplay by Woody Allen and Marshall Brickman. Directed by Woody Allen. Starring Woody Allen, Diane Keaton, Tony Roberts, Carol Kane.

ANOTHER PART OF THE FOREST (1948) Univ. Screenplay by Vladimir Pozner, from a play by Lillian Hellman. Directed by Michael Gordon. Starring Fredric March, Florence Eldridge, Ann Blyth, Dan Duryea.

APARTMENT, THE (1960) UA. Screenplay by Billy Wilder and I.A.L. Diamond. Directed by Billy Wilder. Starring Jack Lemmon, Shirley MacLaine, Fred MacMurray.

APOCALYPSE NOW (1979) UA. Screenplay by John Milius and Francis Ford Coppola, from the novella *Heart of Darkness* by Joseph Conrad. Directed by Francis Ford Coppola. Starring Marlon Brando, Robert Duvall, Martin Sheen.

ARSENIC AND OLD LACE (1944) WB. Screenplay by Julius and Philip Epstein. Based on the play by Joseph Kesselring. Directed by Frank Capra. Starring Cary Grant, Raymond Massey, Peter Lorre, Josephine Hull.

ARTHUR (1982) Ori. Screenplay and directed by Steve Gordon. Starring Dudley Moore, Liza Minnelli, John Gielgud.

ASPHALT JUNGLE, THE (1950) MGM. Screenplay by Ben Maddow and John Huston. Directed by John Huston. Starring Sterling Hayden, Louis Calhern, Sam Jaffe.

AUNTIE MAME (1958) WB. Screenplay by Betty Comden and Adolph Green, from the novel by Patrick Dennis and the play adapted by Jerome Lawrence and Robert E. Lee. Directed by Morton DaCosta. Starring Rosalind Russell, Peggy Cass, Coral Browne.

AUTUMN SONATA (1978) Personafilm. Screenplay and directed by Ingmar Bergman. Starring Ingrid Bergman and Liv Ullmann.

AWFUL TRUTH, THE (1937) Col. Screenplay by Vina Delmar. Based on the play by Arthur Richman. Directed by Leo McCarey. Starring Cary Grant, Irene Dunne, Ralph Bellamy.

BABES IN ARMS (1939) MGM. Screenplay by Jack MacGowan and Kay Van Riper. Based on the musical by Richard Rodgers and Lorenz Hart. Directed by Busby Berkeley. Starring Mickey Rooney and Judy Garland.

BACHELOR AND THE BOBBY-SOXER, THE (1947) RKO. Screenplay by Sidney Sheldon. Directed by Irving Reis. Starring Cary Grant, Myrna Loy, Shirley Temple, Rudy Vallee.

BACHELOR PARTY, THE (1957) UA. Screenplay by Paddy Chayefsky. Directed by Delbert Mann. Starring Don Murray, E.G. Marshall, Jack Warden.

BAD AND THE BEAUTIFUL, THE (1952) MGM. Screenplay by Charles Schnee. Directed by Vincente Minnelli. Starring Lana Turner, Kirk Douglas, Dick Powell, Walter Pidgeon.

BAD SEED, THE (1956) WB. Screenplay by John

Lee Mahon. Based on the play by Maxwell Anderson.
Directed by Mervyn Leroy. Starring Nancy Kelly, Patty
MacCormack, Eileen Heckart, Henry Jones.

BALL OF FIRE (1941) RKO. Screenplay by Charles
Brackett and Billy Wilder. Directed by Howard Hawks.
Starring Gary Cooper and Barbara Stanwyck.

BAND WAGON, THE (1953) MGM. Screenplay by
Betty Comden and Adolph Green. Directed by Vincente
Minnelli. Starring Fred Astaire, Cyd Charisse, Nanette
Fabray, Oscar Levant.

BANG THE DRUM SLOWLY (1982) Par. Screen-
play by Mark Harris, from his novel. Directed by John
Hancock. Starring Robert De Niro, Michael Moriarty,
Vincent Gardenia.

BANK DICK, THE (1940) Univ. Screenplay by
W.C. Fields. Directed by Edward Cline. Starring W.C.
Fields, Una Merkel, Franklin Pangborn.

BAREFOOT CONTESSA, THE (1954) UA. Screenplay and directed by Joseph Mankiewicz. Starring Humphrey Bogart, Ava Gardner, Edmond O'Brien.

BAREFOOT IN THE PARK (1967) Par. Screenplay
by Neil Simon, based on his play. Directed by Gene Saks.
Starring Robert Redford, Jane Fonda, Charles Boyer, Mildred Natwick.

BATMAN (1990) WB. Screenplay by Sam Hamm
and Warren Bkaaren, from a character created by Bob
Kane. Directed by Tim Burton. Starring Michael Keaton
and Jack Nicholson.

BEACH PARTY (1963) AIP. Screenplay by Lou Ru-
soff. Directed by William Asher. Starring Robert Cummings, Dorothy Malone, Frankie Avalon, Annette
Funicello.

BEAT THE DEVIL (1954) UA. Screenplay by John
Huston and Truman Capote. Directed by John Huston.

Starring Humphrey Bogart, Jennifer Jones, Robert Morley, Peter Lorre.

BEAU GESTE (1939) Par. Screenplay by Robert Carson. Based on the novel by Persival Christopher Wren. Starring Gary Cooper, Ray Milland, Robert Preston, Brian Donlevy.

BEAU JAMES (1957) Par. Screenplay by Jack Rose, Melville Shavelson, from a book by Gene Fowler. Directed by Melville Shavelson. Starring Bob Hope, Paul Douglas.

BEING THERE (1979) UA. Screenplay by Jerzy Kosinski, based on his novel. Directed by Hal Ashby. Starring Peter Sellers, Shirley MacLaine, Melvyn Douglas.

BELLE OF THE NINETIES (1934) Par. Screenplay by Mae West. Directed by Leo McCarey. Starring Mae West.

BELLS OF ST. MARY'S, THE (1945) RKO. Screenplay by Dudley Nichols. Directed by Leo McCarey. Starring Bing Crosby and Ingrid Bergman.

BEN-HUR (1959) MGM. Screenplay by Karl Kunburg. Based on the novel by Lew Wallace. Starring Charlton Heston, Jack Hawkins, Stephen Boyd.

BEST MAN, THE (1964) MGM/UA. Screenplay by Gore Vidal, based on his play. Directed by Franklin Schaffner. Starring Henry Fonda, Cliff Robertson.

BEVERLY HILLS COP (1985) Par. Screenplay by Daniel Petrie, Jr. Directed by Martin Brest. Starring Eddie Murphy, Judge Reinhold.

BIG (1989) 20th. Screenplay by Gary Ross and Anne Spielberg. Directed by Penny Marshall. Starring Tom Hanks, Robert Loggia, John Heard.

BIG CARNIVAL, THE see ACE IN THE HOLE.

BIG HEAT, THE (1953) Col. Screenplay by Sydney Boehm. Based on the novel by William P. McGivern.

Directed by Fritz Lang. Starring Glenn Ford, Gloria Grahame, Lee Marvin.

BIG SLEEP, THE (1946) WB. Screenplay by William Faulkner, Leigh Brackett, Jules Furthman. Directed by Howard Hawks. Starring Humphrey Bogart and Lauren Bacall.

BIKINI BEACH (1964) AIP. Screenplay by William Asher, Leo Townsend, Robert Diller. Directed by William Asher. Starring Frankie Avalon, Annette Funicello, Don Rickles, Harvey Lembeck.

BILLY BUDD (1962) AA. Screenplay by Peter Ustinov, Anthony Hopkins. Based on the novel by Herman Melville. Directed by Peter Ustinov. Starring Robert Ryan, Peter Ustinov, Melvyn Douglas, Terence Stamp.

BLADE RUNNER (1983) WB. Screenplay by Hampton Fancher, David Peoples. Based on the novel by Philip Dick. Directed by Ridley Scott. Starring Harrison Ford, Rutger Hauer, Daryl Hannah.

BLAZING SADDLES (1974) WB. Screenplay by Mel Brooks, Norman Steinberg, Andrew Bergman, Richard Pryor, Alan Uger. Directed by Mel Brooks. Starring Cleavon Little, Gene Wilder, Mel Brooks, Madeline Kahn, Harvey Korman.

BLOCKADE (1938) Walter Wanger. Screenplay by John Howard Lawson, Directed by William Dieterle. Starring Henry Fonda, Madeleine Carroll, Leo Carrillo.

BLOWUP (1966) MGM. Screenplay by Michelangelo Antonioni, Tonino Guevra. Directed by Michelangelo Antonioni. Starring David Hemmings, Vanessa Redgrave, Sarah Miles.

BLUEBEARD'S EIGHTH WIFE (1938) Par. Screenplay by Charles Brackett, Billy Wilder, from a play by Alfred Savoir. Directed by Ernst Lubitsch. Starring Claudette Colbert, Gary Cooper, David Niven.

BLUE VELVET (1987) DeLaurentiis Entertainment. Screenplay and directed by David Lynch. Starring Isabella Rossellini, Dennis Hopper, Laura Dern.

BLUME IN LOVE (1973) WB. Screenplay and directed by Paul Mazursky. Starring George Segal, Susan Anspach, Kris Kristofferson.

BOB AND CAROL AND TED AND ALICE (1969) Col. Screenplay by Paul Mazursky and Larry Tucker. Directed by Paul Mazursky. Starring Robert Culp, Natalie Wood, Elliott Gould, Dyan Cannon.

BODY AND SOUL (1947) UA. Screenplay by Abraham Polonsky. Directed by Robert Rossen. Starring John Garfield and Lilli Palmer.

BODY HEAT (1981) WB. Screenplay and directed by Lawrence Kasdan. Starring William Hurt and Kathleen Turner.

BONNIE AND CLYDE (1967) WB-7 Arts. Screenplay by David Newman and Robert Benton. Directed by Arthur Penn. Starring Warren Beatty, Faye Dunaway, Gene Hackman, Estelle Parsons, Michael J. Pollard.

BORN YESTERDAY (1950) Col. Screenplay by Albert Mannheimer, from the play by Garson Kanin. Directed by George Cukor. Starring Judy Holliday, Broderick Crawford, William Holden.

BOYS IN THE BAND, THE (1970) Cinema Center. Screenplay by Mart Crowley from his play. Directed by William Friedkin. Starring Leonard Frey, Cliff Gorman, Laurence Luckinbill.

BOYS TOWN (1938) MGM. Screenplay by John Meehan and Dore Schary. Directed by Norman Taurog. Starring Spencer Tracy and Mickey Rooney.

BREAKFAST AT TIFFANY'S (1961) Par. Screenplay by George Axelrod. Based on the novel by Truman

Capote. Directed by Blake Edwards. Starring Audrey Hepburn, George Peppard, Patricia Neal.

BREAKFAST CLUB, THE (1986) UA. Screenplay and directed by John Hughes. Starring Emilio Estevez, Judd Nelson, Molly Ringwald, Anthony Michael Hall, Ally Sheedy.

BREAKING AWAY (1979) Screenplay by Steven Tesich. Directed by Peter Yates. Starring Dennis Christopher, Paul Dooley, Barbara Barrie.

BRIDE CAME C.O.D., THE (1941) WB. Screenplay by Julius and Philip Epstein. Directed by William Keighley. Starring Bette Davis, James Cagney, Jack Carson.

BRIDE OF FRANKENSTEIN (1935) Univ. Screenplay by John Balderston and William Hurlbut. Directed by James Whale. Starring Boris Karloff, Colin Clive, Elsa Lanchester.

BRIDE WALKS OUT, THE (1936) RKO. Screenplay by P.J. Wolfson, Philip Epstein. Directed by Leigh Jason. Starring Barbara Stanwyck, Robert Young.

BRIDGE ON THE RIVER KWAI, THE (1957) Col. Screenplay by Carl Foreman and Michael Wilson. Based on the novel by Pierre Boulle. Directed by David Lean. Starring William Holden, Alec Guinness, Sessue Hayakawa.

BRIGHT LIGHTS, BIG CITY (1989) UA. Screenplay by Jay McInerney, based on his novel. Directed by James Bridges. Starring Michael J. Fox, Kiefer Sutherland.

BRIGHTON BEACH MEMOIRS (1987) Univ. Screenplay by Neil Simon, based on his play. Directed by Gene Saks. Starring Jonathan Silverman, Blythe Danner, Bob Dishy.

BROADCAST NEWS (1987) 20th. Screenplay and

directed by James L. Brooks. Starring William Hurt, Holly Hunter, Albert Brooks.

BROADWAY DANNY ROSE (1985) Ori. Screenplay and directed by Woody Allen. Starring Woody Allen, Mia Farrow, Nick Apollo Forte.

BUDDY BUDDY (1982) MGM/UA. Screenplay by Billy Wilder and I.A.L. Diamond, from a play and film by Francis Veber. Directed by Billy Wilder. Starring Jack Lemmon, Walter Matthau, Paula Prentiss, Klaus Kinski.

BULL DURHAM (1989) Ori. Screenplay and directed by Ron Shelton. Starring Susan Sarandon, Kevin Costner, Tim Robbins.

BUTCH CASSIDY AND THE SUNDANCE KID (1969) 20th. Screenplay by William Goldman. Directed by George Roy Hill. Starring Paul Newman, Robert Redford, Katharine Ross.

BUTTERFIELD 8 (1960) MGM. Screenplay by Charles Schnee and John Michael Hayes. Based on the novel by John O'Hara. Directed by Daniel Mann. Starring Elizabeth Taylor, Laurence Harvey, Eddie Fisher.

CABARET (1972) AA. Screenplay by Jay Presson Allen. Based on the musical play by Joe Masteroff, the play by John Van Druten, and the book by Christopher Isherwood. Directed by Bob Fosse. Starring Liza Minnelli, Michael York, Joel Grey.

CABIN IN THE COTTON (1932) WB. Screenplay by Paul Green, from the novel by Harry Knoll. Directed by Michael Curtiz. Starring Richard Barthelmess, Bette Davis.

CACTUS FLOWER (1969) Col. Screenplay by I.A.L. Diamond, from the play by Abe Burrows, based on the French play by Barillet and Gredy. Directed by Gene Saks. Starring Walter Matthau, Ingrid Bergman, Goldie Hawn.

CAINE MUTINY, THE (1954) Col. Screenplay by Stanley Roberts. Based on the novel by Herman Wouk. Directed by Edward Dmytryk. Starring Humphrey Bogart, Jose Ferrer, Van Johnson, Fred MacMurray.

CALIFORNIA SUITE (1989) Col. Screenplay by Neil Simon. Directed by Herbert Ross. Starring Alan Alda, Michael Caine, Bill Cosby, Jane Fonda, Walter Matthau, Elaine May, Richard Pryor, Maggie Smith.

CALL ME MADAM (1953) 20th. Screenplay by Arthur Sheekman. Based on the musical by Howard Lindsay and Russell Crouse. Directed by Walter Lang. Starring Ethel Merman, Donald O'Connor, George Sanders, Vera-Ellen.

CAMILLE (1936) MGM. Screenplay by Zoe Akins, Frances Marion, James Hilton. Based on the novel by Alexandre Dumas. Directed by George Cukor. Starring Greta Garbo, Robert Taylor, Lionel Barrymore.

CARNAL KNOWLEDGE (1971) Avco Embassy. Screenplay by Jules Feiffer. Directed by Mike Nichols. Starring Jack Nicholson, Ann-Margret, Art Garfunkel, Candice Bergen.

CASABLANCA (1942) WB. Screenplay by Julius and Philip Epstein. Based on an unproduced play by Murray Burnett and Joan Alison. Directed by Michael Curtiz. Starring Humphrey Bogart, Ingrid Bergman, Paul Henreid, Claude Rains, Peter Lorre, Sydney Greenstreet.

CAT AND THE CANARY, THE (1979) Gala. Screenplay and directed by Radley Metzger. Starring Honor Blackman and Michael Callan.

CATCH-22 (1979) Par. Screenplay by Buck Henry, from the novel by Joseph Heller. Directed by Mike Nichols. Starring Alan Arkin, Martin Balsam, Richard Benjamin, Arthur Garfunkel, Jack Gilford, Orson Welles.

CAT ON A HOT TIN ROOF (1958) MGM. Screenplay by Richard Brooks and James Poe. Based on the play by Tennessee Williams. Directed by Richard Brooks. Starring Elizabeth Taylor, Paul Newman, Burl Ives, Jack Carson, Judith Anderson.

CHALK GARDEN, THE (1964) Univ. Screenplay by John Michael Hayes, from the play by Enid Bagnold. Directed by Ronald Neame. Starring Edith Evans, Deborah Kerr.

CHAMPION (1949) UA. Screenplay by Carl Foreman, from a story by Ring Lardner. Directed by Mark Robson. Starring Kirk Douglas, Arthur Kennedy, Marilyn Maxwell, Paul Stewart.

CHARADE (1963) Univ. Screenplay by Peter Stone. Directed by Stanley Donen. Starring Cary Grant, Audrey Hepburn, Walter Matthau, James Coburn, George Kennedy.

CHINATOWN (1974) Par. Screenplay by Robert Towne. Directed by Roman Polanski. Starring Jack Nicholson, Faye Dunaway, John Huston.

CITIZEN KANE (1941) RKO. Screenplay by Herman Mankiewicz and Orson Welles. Directed by Orson Welles. Starring Orson Welles, Joseph Cotten, Everett Sloane, Paul Stewart.

CLEOPATRA (1963) 20th. Screenplay by Joseph Mankiewicz, Ranald MacDougall, Sidney Buchman. Directed by Joseph Mankiewicz. Starring Elizabeth Taylor, Richard Burton, Rex Harrison.

COCKTAIL (1987) Tou. Screenplay by Heywood Gould, based on his novel. Directed by Roger Donaldson. Starring Tom Cruise and Bryan Brown.

COCOANUTS, THE (1929) Par. Screenplay by George S. Kaufman, Morrie Ryskind. Directed by Robert Florey and Joseph Santley. Starring Groucho, Chico, Harpo, and Zeppo Marx, Margaret Dumont.

COCOON (1986) 20th. Screenplay by Tom Benedek, from a novel by David Saperstein. Directed by Ron Howard. Starring Don Ameche, Jessica Tandy, Hume Cronyn, Jack Gilford, Gwen Verdon.

COLOR OF MONEY, THE (1987) Tou. Screenplay by Richard Price. Based on the novel by Walter Tevis. Directed by Martin Scorsese. Starring Paul Newman, Tom Cruise, Mary Elizabeth Mastrantonio.

COME BACK, LITTLE SHEBA (1952) Par. Screenplay by Ketti Frings. Based on the play by William Inge. Directed by Daniel Mann. Starring Burt Lancaster and Shirley Booth.

COME FILL THE CUP (1951) WB. Screenplay by Ivan Goff, Ben Roberts, Noel Harlan Ware. Directed by Gordon Douglas. Starring James Cagney, Raymond Massey.

CONQUEROR, THE (1956) RKO. Screenplay by Oscar Millard. Directed by Dick Powell. Starring John Wayne and Susan Hayward.

CONTINENTAL DIVIDE (1982) Univ. Screenplay by Lawrence Kasdan. Directed by Michael Apted. Starring John Belushi, Blair Brown, Allen Goorwitz.

COOL HAND LUKE (1967) WB. Screenplay by Don Pearce and Frank Pierson. Based on the novel by Don Pearce. Directed by Stuart Rosenberg. Starring Paul Newman, George Kennedy, Strother Martin.

COUNTRY GIRL, THE (1954) Par. Screenplay and directed by George Seaton. Based on the play by Clifford Odets. Starring Bing Crosby, Grace Kelly, William Holden.

COURT JESTER, THE (1956) Par. Screenplay by Norman Panama and Melvin Frank. Directed by Norman Panama and Melvin Frank. Starring Danny Kaye, Glynis Johns, Basil Rathbone.

CRIMES AND MISDEMEANORS (1990) Ori. Screenplay and directed by Woody Allen. Starring Martin Landau, Claire Bloom, Woody Allen, Alan Alda, Mia Farrow.

CRIMES OF THE HEART (1986) Lorimar. Screenplay by Beth Henley, based on her play. Directed by Bruce Beresford. Starring Diane Keaton, Sissy Spacek, Jessica Lange.

CROCODILE DUNDEE (1987) Par. Screenplay by Paul Hogan, Ken Shadie, John Cornell. Directed by Peter Faiman. Starring Paul Hogan, Linda Kozlowski.

CROSSROADS (1987) Col. Screenplay by John Fusco. Directed by Walter Hill. Starring Ralph Macchio and Joe Seneca.

CYRANO DE BERGERAC (1950) UA. Screenplay by Carl Foreman. Based on the play by Edmond Rostand. Directed by Michael Gordon. Starring Jose Ferrer, William Prince, Mala Powers.

DAMN YANKEES (1958) WB. Screenplay by George Abbott. Based on the novel by Douglas Wallop and the musical by Abbott. Directed by George Abbott and Stanley Donen. Starring Gwen Verdon, Tab Hunter, Ray Walston.

DANGEROUS LIAISONS (1989) Lorimar. Screenplay by Christopher Hampton, based on his play, from the novel by Pierre Choderlos de Laclos. Directed by Stephen Frears. Starring John Malkovich, Glenn Close, Michelle Pfeiffer.

DARK AT THE TOP OF THE STAIRS, THE (1960) WB. Screenplay by Harriet Frank, Jr. and Irving Ravetch, based on the play by William Inge. Directed by Delbert Mann. Starring Robert Preston, Dorothy McGuire, Eve Arden.

DARK CORNER, THE (1946) 20th. Screenplay by

Jay Dratler, Bernard Schoenfeld. Directed by Henry Hathaway. Starring Mark Stevens, Clifton Webb, Lucille Ball.

DARK VICTORY (1939) WB. Screenplay by Casey Robinson. Directed by Edmund Goulding. Starring Bette Davis, George Brent, Humphrey Bogart, Geraldine Fitzgerald, Ronald Reagan.

DARLING (1965) Embassy. Screenplay by Frederic Raphael. Directed by John Schlesinger. Starring Julie Christie, Laurence Harvey, Dirk Bogarde.

DAY AT THE RACES, A (1937) MGM. Screenplay by Robert Pirosh, George Seaton, George Oppenheimer. Directed by Sam Wood. Starring Groucho, Chico, Harpo Marx, Allan Jones, Maureen O'Sullivan.

DAYS OF WINE AND ROSES (1962) WB. Screenplay by J.P. Miller. Directed by Blake Edwards. Starring Jack Lemmon, Lee Remick, Charles Bickford, Jack Klugman.

DEAD POETS SOCIETY (1990) Tou. Screenplay by Tom Schulman. Directed by Peter Weir. Starring Robin Williams.

DEATH OF A SALESMAN (1951) Col. Screenplay by Stanley Roberts, from the play by Arthur Miller. Directed by Laslo Benedek. Starring Fredric March, Mildred Dunnock, Kevin McCarthy, Cameron Mitchell.

DEER HUNTER, THE (1978) Univ. Screenplay by Deric Washburn. Directed by Michael Cimino. Starring Robert De Niro, John Cazale, Christopher Walken, Meryl Streep, John Savage.

DELICATE BALANCE, A (1975) American Express. Written by Edward Albee, from his play. Directed by Tony Richardson. Starring Katharine Hepburn, Paul Scofield.

DESK SET, THE (1957) 20th. Screenplay by Phoebe

and Henry Ephron, from the play by William Marchant. Directed by Walter Lang. Starring Spencer Tracy and Katharine Hepburn.

DESTINATION TOKYO (1943) WB. Screenplay by Delmer Daves and Albert Maltz. Directed by Delmer Daves. Starring Cary Grant, John Garfield, Alan Hale, Dane Clark.

DETECTIVE STORY (1951) Par. Screenplay by Philip Yordan and Robert Wyler, from the play by Sidney Kingsley. Directed by William Wyler. Starring Kirk Douglas, Eleanor Parker, William Bendix.

DEVIL'S PLAYGROUND, THE (1976) Feature Film House. Written and directed by Fred Schepsi. Starring Arthur Dignam, Nick Tate.

DIAL M FOR MURDER (1954) WB. Screenplay by Frederick Knott, adapted from his play. Directed by Alfred Hitchcock. Starring Ray Milland, Grace Kelly, Robert Cummings, John Williams.

DIARY OF ANNE FRANK, THE (1959) 20th. Screenplay by Frances Goodrich and Albert Hackett. Directed by George Stevens. Starring Millie Perkins, Joseph Schildkraut, Shelley Winters, Ed Wynn, Richard Beymer.

DINNER AT EIGHT (1933) MGM. Screenplay by Frances Marion and Herman Mankiewicz. Based on the play by George S. Kaufman and Edna Ferber. Directed by George Cukor. Starring Marie Dressler, John Barrymore, Wallace Beery, Jean Harlow.

DIRTY DOZEN, THE (1967) MGM. Screenplay by Nunnally Johnson and Lukas Heller. Based on the novel by E.M. Nathanson. Directed by Robert Aldrich. Starring Lee Marvin, Ernest Borgnine, Charles Bronson, Jim Brown, John Cassavetes, George Kennedy, Donald Sutherland, Robert Ryan.

DIRTY HARRY (1971) WB. Screenplay by Harry Julian Fink and Dean Riesner. Directed by Don Siegel. Starring Clint Eastwood, Harry Guardino, Reni Santoni.

DOCTOR ZHIVAGO (1965) MGM. Screenplay by Robert Bolt. Based on the novel by Boris Pasternak. Directed by David Lean. Starring Omar Sharif, Rod Steiger, Tom Courtenay, Geraldine Chaplin, Julie Christie, Alec Guinness.

DOG DAY AFTERNOON (1975) WB. Screenplay by Frank Pierson. Based on a true incident. Directed by Sidney Lumet. Starring Al Pacino, John Cazale, Charles Durning, Carol Kane.

DOUBLE INDEMNITY (1944) Par. Screenplay by Billy Wilder and Raymond Chandler, from a novel by James M. Cain. Directed by Billy Wilder. Starring Fred MacMurray, Barbara Stanwyck, Edward G. Robinson.

DRACULA (1931) Univ. Screenplay by Garrett Fort. Based on the novel by Bram Stoker. Directed by Tod Browning. Starring Bela Lugosi.

DR. JEKYLL AND MR. HYDE (1932) Par. Screenplay by Samuel Hoppenstein and Percy Heath. Based on the story by Robert Louis Stevenson. Directed by Rouben Mamoulian. Starring Fredric March and Miriam Hopkins.

DR. STRANGELOVE (1964) Col. Screenplay by Stanley Kubrick and Terry Southern. Directed by Stanley Kubrick. Starring Peter Sellers, George C. Scott, Sterling Hayden, Keenan Wynn.

DUCK SOUP (1933) Par. Screenplay by Bert Kalmar, Harry Ruby, Arthur Sheekman, Nat Perrin. Directed by Leo McCarey. Starring Groucho, Chico, Harpo, and Zeppo Marx, Margaret Dumont.

DUEL IN THE SUN (1946) Selznick Releasing Organization. Screenplay by David O. Selznick. Based on the novel by Niven Busch. Directed by King Vidor. Starring Jennifer Jones, Joseph Cotten, Gregory Peck, Lionel Barrymore, Walter Huston.

DUNE (1985) Univ. Screenplay by David Lynch, from the novel by Frank Herbert. Directed by David Lynch. Starring Kyle MacLachlan, Jose Ferrer, Kenneth McMillan, Dean Stockwell.

ELENI (1986) WB. Screenplay by Steven Tesich, from the novel by Nicolas Gage. Directed by Peter Yates. Starring John Malkovich, Kate Nelligan, Linda Hunt.

ELEPHANT MAN, THE (1980) EMI. Screenplay by Christopher de Core, Eric Bergren, based on various memoirs. Directed by David Lynch. Starring Anthony Hopkins, John Hurt, John Gielgud.

EMERALD FOREST, THE (1986) Embassy. Screenplay by Rospo Pallenberg. Directed by John Boorman. Starring Powers Boothe, Charley Boorman.

E.T. THE EXTRA-TERRESTRIAL (1983) Univ. Screenplay by Melissa Mathieson. Directed by Steven Spielberg. Starring Henry Thomas, Drew Barrymore, Peter Coyote.

EXORCIST, THE (1973) WB. Screenplay by William Peter Blatty, based on his novel. Directed by William Friedkin. Starring Ellen Burstyn, Linda Blair, Jason Miller, Lee J. Cobb, Max von Sydow.

FAREWELL, MY LOVELY (1975) Screenplay by David Zelag Goodman, from the novel by Raymond Chandler. Directed by Dick Richards. Starring Robert Mitchum, Charlotte Rampling, John Ireland.

FAREWELL TO ARMS, A (1932) Par. Screenplay by Benjamin Glazer and Oliver H.P. Garrett. Based on the novel by Ernest Hemingway. Directed by Frank Borzage. Starring Helen Hayes and Gary Cooper.

FATHER GOOSE (1964) Univ. Screenplay by Peter Stone. Directed by Ralph Nelson. Starring Cary Grant, Leslie Caron, Trevor Howard.

FEMALE ON THE BEACH, THE (1955) Univ. Screenplay by Robert Hill, Richard Alan Simmons. Directed by Joseph Pevney. Starring Joan Crawford, Jeff Chandler.

FIDDLER ON THE ROOF (1971) UA. Screenplay by Joseph Stein, based on his book for the musical. Directed by Norman Jewison. Starring Topol, Norma Crane, Leonard Frey, Molly Picon.

FIELD OF DREAMS (1990) Univ. Screenplay by Phil Alden Robinson, from a novel by W.P. Kinsella. Directed by Phil Alden Robinson. Starring Kevin Costner, James Earl Jones, Burt Lancaster.

FINIAN'S RAINBOW (1968) WB. Screenplay by E.Y. Harburg and Fred Saidy, based on their musical. Directed by Francis Ford Coppola. Starring Fred Astaire, Keenan Wynn, Al Freeman, Jr.

FIRE DOWN BELOW (1957) Col. Screenplay by Irwin Shaw. Based on a novel by Max Catto. Directed by Robert Parrish. Starring Rita Hayworth, Robert Mitchum.

FIRST MONDAY IN OCTOBER (1981) Par. Screenplay by Jerome Lawrence and Robert E. Lee, based on their play. Directed by Ronald Neame. Starring Walter Matthau and Jill Clayburgh.

FIRST NAME: CARMEN (1985) Spectra Film. Screenplay by Anne-Marie Mieville. Directed by Jean-Luc Godard. Starring Masruschka Detmers, Jacques Bonnaffe.

FISH CALLED WANDA, A (1989) MGM-UA. Screenplay by John Cleese. Directed by Charles Crichton. Starring Jamie Lee Curtis, Kevin Kline, John Cleese.

FIVE EASY PIECES (1970) Col. Screenplay by Adrien Joyce, from a story by Bob Rafelson and Adrien Joyce. Directed by Bob Rafelson. Starring Jack Nicholson and Karen Black.

FIVE PENNIES, THE (1959) Par. Screenplay by Jack Rose and Melville Shavelson. Directed by Melville Shavelson. Starring Danny Kaye, Barbara Bel Geddes, Louis Armstrong.

FLETCH (1986) Univ. Screenplay by Andrew Bergman, from the novel by Gregory MacDonald. Directed by Michael Ritchie. Starring Chevy Chase, Joe Don Baker, George Wendt, Richard Libertini.

FLY, THE (1958) 20th. Screenplay by James Clavell. Directed by Kurt Neumann. Starring Al Hedison, Patricia Owens, Vincent Price, Herbert Marshall.

FOOTLIGHT PARADE (1933) WB. Screenplay by Manuel Seff, James Seymour. Directed by Lloyd Bacon. Starring James Cagney, Joan Blondell, Ruby Keeler, Dick Powell.

FORCE OF EVIL (1948) MGM. Screenplay by Abraham Polonsky, from the novel by Ira Wolfert. Starring John Garfield, Beatrice Pearson, Thomas Gomez.

FOREIGN AFFAIR, A (1948) Par. Screenplay by Charles Brackett, Billy Wilder, Richard Breen. Directed by Billy Wilder. Starring Jean Arthur, Marlene Dietrich, John Lund.

FOREIGN CORRESPONDENT (1940) UA. Screenplay by Charles Brackett and Joan Harrison. Directed by Alfred Hitchcock. Starring Joel McCrea, Loraine Day, George Sanders.

FORTUNE COOKIE, THE (1966) UA. Screenplay by Billy Wilder and I.A.L. Diamond. Directed by Billy Wilder. Starring Walter Matthau, Jack Lemmon.

42ND STREET (1933) WB. Screenplay by James Seymour, Rean James, from the novel by Bradford Roper.

Directed by Lloyd Bacon. Starring Warner Baxter, Bebe Daniels, George Brent, Ruby Keeler, Dick Powell.

FOR WHOM THE BELL TOLLS (1943) Par. Screenplay by Dudley Nichols. Based on the novel by Ernest Hemingway. Directed by Sam Wood. Starring Gary Cooper, Ingrid Bergman, Akim Tamiroff.

FOUR DAUGHTERS (1938) WB. Screenplay by Julius Epstein, Lenore Coffee. Directed by Michael Curtiz. Starring Claude Rains, Priscilla Lane, John Garfield, Rosemary Lane, Lola Lane.

FRANKENSTEIN (1931) Univ. Screenplay by Garrett Fort and Francis Faragoh. Directed by James Whale. Starring Colin Clive, Mae Clarke, Boris Karloff.

FRENCH LINE, THE (1953) RKO. Screenplay by Mary Loos and Richard Sale. Directed by Lloyd Bacon. Starring Jane Russell, Gilbert Roland.

FROM HERE TO ETERNITY (1953) Col. Screenplay by Daniel Taradash, from the novel by James Jones. Directed by Fred Zinnemann. Starring Burt Lancaster, Montgomery Clift, Deborah Kerr, Frank Sinatra, Donna Reed, Ernest Borgnine.

FRONT PAGE, THE (1931) UA. Screenplay by Bartlett Cormack and Charles Lederer, from the play by Ben Hecht and Charles MacArthur. Directed by Lewis Milestone. Starring Adolphe Menjou and Pat O'Brien.

FUNNY FACE (1957) Par. Screenplay by Leonard Beishe. Directed by Stanley Donen. Starring Audrey Hepburn and Fred Astaire.

FUNNY GIRL (1968) Col. Screenplay by Isobel Lennart, based on her musical. Directed by William Wyler. Starring Barbra Streisand, Omar Sharif, Walter Pidgeon, Kay Medford.

FUNNY THING HAPPENED ON THE WAY TO THE FORUM, A (1966) UA. Screenplay by Melvin Frank and Michael Pertwei. Based on the musical book by Burt Shevelove and Larry Gelbart. Directed by Richard Lester. Starring Zero Mostel, Phil Silvers, Jack Gilford.

GAY DIVORCEE, THE (1931) RKO. Screenplay by George Marion, Jr., Dorothy Yost, Edward Kaufman. Directed by Mark Sandrich. Starring Fred Astaire, Ginger Rogers, Edward Everett Horton.

GENTLEMEN PREFER BLONDES (1953) 20th. Screenplay by Charles Lederer. Directed by Howard Hawks. Starring Jane Russell, Marilyn Monroe, Charles Coburn.

GENTLEMEN'S AGREEMENT (1947) 20th. Screenplay by Moss Hart. Based on the novel by Laura Z. Hobson. Directed by Elia Kazan. Starring Gregory Peck, Dorothy McGuire, John Garfield, Celeste Holm.

GEORGY GIRL (1966) Col. Screenplay by Margaret Foster, Peter Nichols, from the novel by Margaret Foster. Directed by Silvio Narizzano. Starring James Mason, Lynn Redgrave, Charlotte Rampling, Alan Bates.

GHOST AND MRS. MUIR, THE (1947) 20th. Screenplay by Philip Dunne, from the novel by R.A. Dick. Directed by Joseph Mankiewicz. Starring Gene Tierney, Rex Harrison, George Sanders.

GHOST BREAKERS, THE (1940) Par. Screenplay by Paul Dickey, Walter de Leon, from a play by Paul Dickey. Starring Bob Hope, Paulette Goddard, Paul Lukas.

GHOSTBUSTERS (1985) Col. Screenplay by Dan Aykroyd, Harold Ramis. Directed by Ivan Reitman. Starring Bill Murray, Dan Aykroyd, Sigourney Weaver, Harold Ramis, Rick Moranis.

GIANT (1956) WB. Screenplay by Fred Guiol. Based on the novel by Edna Ferber. Directed by George Stevens.

Starring Elizabeth Taylor, Rock Hudson, James Dean, Dennis Hopper.

GIGI (1958) MGM. Screenplay by Alan Jay Lerner, from the novel by Colette. Directed by Vincente Minnelli. Starring Leslie Caron, Maurice Chevalier, Louis Jourdan, Hermoine Gingold.

GIRL HAPPY (1965) MGM. Screenplay by Harvey Bullock and R.S. Allen. Directed by Boris Sagal. Starring Elvis Presley, Gary Crosby, Harold Stone, Jackie Coogan.

GLASS MENAGERIE, THE (1988) Uniplex Odeon. Written by Tennessee Williams. Directed by Paul Newman. Starring Joanne Woodward, John Malkovich, Karen Allen.

GO-BETWEEN, THE (1971) Screenplay by Harold Pinter, from the novel by L. P. Hartley. Directed by Joseph Losey. Starring Julie Christie, Michael Redgrave, Alan Bates, Dominic Guard.

GODDESS, THE (1958) Col. Screenplay by Paddy Chayefsky. Directed by John Cromwell. Starring Kim Stanley, Joyce Van Patten, Lloyd Bridges.

GODFATHER, THE (1972) Par. Screenplay by Mario Puzo and Francis Ford Coppola. Based on the novel by Mario Puzo. Directed by Francis Ford Coppola. Starring Marlon Brando, Al Pacino, James Caan, Robert Duvall, Sterling Hayden, Diane Keaton, Talia Shire, John Cazale.

GODFATHER II (1974) Par. Screenplay by Mario Puzo and Francis Ford Coppola. Based on the novel by Mario Puzo. Directed by Francis Ford Coppola. Starring Robert De Niro, Al Pacino, Robert Duvall, Diane Keaton, Talia Shire.

GOING MY WAY (1944) Par. Screenplay by Frank Butler and Frank Cavett. Directed by Leo McCarey. Starring Bing Crosby, Rise Stevens, Barry Fitzgerald.

GOLD DIGGERS OF 1933 (1933) WB. Screenplay by Erwin Gelsey, James Seymour. Based on the play by Avery Hopwood. Directed by Mervyn Leroy. Starring Warren William, Joan Blondell, Ruby Keeler, Ned Sparks.

GOLDEN BOY (1939) Col. Screenplay by Lewis Meltzer, Daniel Taradash, Sarah Mason, Victor Herman, from the play by Clifford Odets. Directed by Rouben Mamoulian. Starring William Holden, Barbara Stanwyck.

GOLDFINGER (1964) UA. Screenplay by Richard Maibaum and Paul Dehn. Based on the novel by Ian Fleming. Directed by Guy Hamilton. Starring Sean Connery, Gert Frobe, Honor Blackman.

GONE WITH THE WIND (1939) MGM. A Selznick International Picture. Screenplay by Sidney Howard, from the novel by Margaret Mitchell. Directed by Victor Fleming, Sam Wood, George Cukor. Starring Vivien Leigh, Clark Gable, Olivia de Havilland, Leslie Howard.

GOODBYE GIRL, THE (1977) WB. Written by Neil Simon. Directed by Herbert Ross. Starring Richard Dreyfuss and Marsha Mason.

GOODBYE, MR. CHIPS (1939) MGM. Screenplay by R.C. Sherriff, from the novel by James Hilton. Directed by Sam Wood. Starring Robert Donat and Greer Garson.

GOOD MORNING, VIETNAM (1987) Tou. Screenplay by Mitch Markowitz. Directed by Barry Levinson. Starring Robin Williams and Bruno Kirby.

GOOD, THE BAD AND THE UGLY, THE (1966) PEA. Screenplay by Age Scarpelli, Luciano Vincenzoni, Sergio Leone. Directed by Sergio Leone. Starring Clint Eastwood, Eli Wallach, Lee Van Cleef.

GO WEST, YOUNG MAN (1936) Par. Screenplay by Mae West. Directed by Henry Hathaway. Starring Mae West, Randolph Scott, Warren William.

GRADUATE, THE (1967) Embassy. Screenplay by Calder Willingham and Buck Henry, from the novel by Charles Webb. Directed by Mike Nichols. Starring Dustin Hoffman, Anne Bancroft, Katharine Ross, William Daniels, Murray Hamilton.

GRAND HOTEL (1932) MGM. Screenplay by William Drake, from the play by Vicki Baum. Directed by Edmund Goulding. Starring Greta Garbo, John Barrymore, Joan Crawford, Wallace Beery, Lionel Barrymore, Lewis Stone.

GRAPES OF WRATH, THE (1940) 20th. Screenplay by Nunnally Johnson. Based on the novel by John Steinbeck. Directed by John Ford. Starring Henry Fonda, Jane Darwell, John Carradine.

GRASSHOPPER, THE (1969) National General Pictures. Screenplay by Jerry Belson, from the novel by Mark MacShane. Directed by Jerry Paris. Starring Jacqueline Bisset, Jim Brown, Joseph Cotten.

GREAT MUPPET CAPER, THE (1982) Univ. Screenplay by Tom Patchett, Jay Tarses, Jerry Juhl, Jack Rose. Directed by Jim Henson. Starring Diana Rigg, Charles Grodin, Jack Warden, Robert Morley.

GREAT ZIEGFELD, THE (1936) MGM. Screenplay by William Anthony McGuire. Directed by Robert Z. Leonard. Starring William Powell, Luise Rainer, Myrna Loy.

GREEN BERETS, THE (1968) WB-7 Arts. Screenplay by James Lee Barrett. Directed by John Wayne and Ray Kellogg. Starring John Wayne, David Janssen, Jim Hutton.

GREEN YEARS, THE (1946) MGM. Screenplay by Robert Artrey, Sonya Levien, from the novel by A.J. Cronin. Directed by Victor Saville. Starring Charles Coburn, Tom Drake, Dean Stockwell, Hume Cronyn.

GREMLINS (1985) WB. Screenplay by Chris Columbus. Directed by Joe Dante. Starring Phoebe Cates, Zach Galligan, Hoyt Axton.

GREYSTOKE: THE LEGEND OF TARZAN (1985) WB. Screenplay by P.H. Vazak, Michael Astin, from the novel by Edgar Rice Burroughs. Directed by Hugh Hudson. Starring Christopher Lambert, Ralph Richardson, Ian Holm.

GUESS WHO'S COMING TO DINNER (1967) Col. Screenplay by William Rose. Directed by Stanley Kramer. Starring Spencer Tracy, Katharine Hepburn, Sidney Poitier.

GUNFIGHT AT THE O.K. CORRAL (1957) Par. Screenplay by Leon Uris. Directed by John Sturges. Starring Burt Lancaster, Kirk Douglas, Rhonda Fleming.

GUNGA DIN (1939) RKO. Screenplay by Joel Sayre, Fred Guiol. Based on the poem by Rudyard Kipling. Directed by George Stevens. Starring Cary Grant, Victor McLaglen, Douglas Fairbanks, Jr., Sam Jaffe, Joan Fontaine.

GUNS IN THE TREES (1961) FC Films. Screenplay and directed by Jonas Mekas. Starring Ben Carruthers, Frances Stillman.

GUY NAMED JOE, A (1943) MGM. Screenplay by Dalton Trumbo. Directed by Victor Fleming. Starring Spencer Tracy, Irene Dunne, Van Johnson.

GUYS AND DOLLS (1955) MGM. Screenplay by Joseph Mankiewicz. Based on the musical by Jo Swerling and Abe Burrows. Directed by Joseph Mankiewicz. Starring Marlon Brando, Jean Simmons, Frank Sinatra, Vivian Blaine.

HAIL THE CONQUERING HERO (1944) Par. Screenplay and directed by Preston Sturges. Starring Eddie Bracken, Ella Raines, William Demarest.

HALLOWEEN II (1982) Univ. Screenplay and directed by Tommy Lee Wallace. Starring Tom Atkins, Stacy Nelkin.

HANNAH AND HER SISTERS (1987) Ori. Screenplay and directed by Woody Allen. Starring Mia Farrow, Woody Allen, Dianne Wiest, Carrie Fisher, Barbara Hershey, Michael Caine.

HAROLD AND MAUDE (1971) Par. Screenplay by Colin Higgins. Directed by Hal Ashby. Starring Bud Cort and Ruth Gordon.

HARPER (1966) WB. Screenplay by William Goldman. Based on the novel by Ross Macdonald. Directed by Jack Smight. Starring Paul Newman, Lauren Bacall, Julie Harris, Arthur Hill, Robert Wagner.

HARRY AND TONTO (1974) 20th. Screenplay by Paul Mazursky and Josh Greenfeld. Directed by Paul Mazursky. Starring Art Carney, Ellen Burstyn.

HARVEY (1950) Univ. Screenplay by Mary C. Chase, based on her play. Directed by Henry Koster. Starring James Stewart and Josephine Hull.

HASTY HEART, THE (1949) ABP. Screenplay by Ranald MacDougall, from the play by John Patrick. Directed by Vincent Sherman. Starring Richard Todd, Patricia Neal, Ronald Reagan.

HEALTH (1979) TCF. Screenplay by Robert Altman, Paul Dooley, Frank Barhydt. Directed by Robert Altman. Starring Lauren Bacall, Glenda Jackson, Dick Cavett.

HEARTBREAK KID, THE (1972) Screenplay by Neil Simon, from a story by Bruce Jay Friedman. Directed by Elaine May. Starring Charles Grodin, Cybill Shepherd, Jeannie Berlin, Eddie Albert.

HEAT'S ON, THE (1943) Col. Screenplay by Fitzroy

Davis, George S. George, Fred Schiller. Directed by Gregory Ratoff. Starring Mae West, Victor Moore.

HEIRESS, THE (1949) Par. Screenplay by Ruth and August Goetz, based on their play, suggested by the novel *Washington Square* by Henry James. Directed by William Wyler. Starring Olivia de Havilland, Montgomery Clift, Ralph Richardson.

HELLO, DOLLY! (1968) 20th. Screenplay by Ernest Lehman. Based on the musical by Michael Stewart and the play by Thornton Wilder. Directed by Gene Kelly. Starring Barbra Streisand, Walter Matthau, Michael Crawford, Louis Armstrong.

HELLZAPOPPIN (1942) Univ. Screenplay by Nat Perrin, Warren Wilson. Directed by H.C. Potter. Starring Ole Olsen, Chic Johnson, Hugh Herbert, Martha Raye.

HERE COMES MR. JORDAN (1941) Col. Screenplay by Seton Miller, from the play by Henry Segall. Directed by Alexander Hall. Starring Robert Montgomery, Evelyn Keyes, Claude Rains.

HIGH NOON (1952) UA. Screenplay by Carl Foreman, from a story by John Cunningham. Directed by Fred Zinnemann. Starring Gary Cooper, Grace Kelly, Lloyd Bridges, Thomas Mitchell.

HIS GIRL FRIDAY (1940) Col. Screenplay by Charles Lederer, from the play by Ben Hecht and Charles MacArthur. Starring Cary Grant, Rosalind Russell, Ralph Bellamy.

HISTORY OF THE WORLD—PART I (1981) Brooksfilms. Screenplay and directed by Mel Brooks. Starring Mel Brooks, Dom De Luise, Madeline Kahn, Cloris Leachman.

HOLIDAY (1938) RKO-Pathé. Screenplay by Donald Ogden Stewart and Sidney Buchman, from the play by

Philip Barry. Directed by George Cukor. Starring Katharine Hepburn, Cary Grant, Lew Ayres.

HOPE AND GLORY (1988) Col. Screenplay and directed by John Boorman. Starring Sarah Miles, David Hayman, Sebastian Rice-Edwards.

HORSE FEATHERS (1932) Par. Screenplay by Bert Kalmar, Harry Ruby, S.J. Perelman, Will B. Johnstone. Directed by Norman Z. McLeon. Starring Groucho, Chico, Harpo, and Zeppo Marx, Thelma Todd.

HOSPITAL, THE (1971) UA. Screenplay by Paddy Chayefsky. Directed by Arthur Hiller. Starring George C. Scott, Diana Rigg, Barnard Hughes.

HOUND OF THE BASKERVILLES, THE (1982) Screenplay by Peter Cook, Dudley Moore, and Paul Mazursky, from the novel by Arthur Conan Doyle. Directed by Paul Mazursky. Starring Peter Cook, Dudley Moore, Denholm Elliott.

HOW GREEN WAS MY VALLEY (1941) 20th. Screenplay by Philip Dunne from the novel by Richard Llewellyn. Directed by John Ford. Starring Walter Pidgeon, Maureen O'Hara, Donald Crisp, Roddy McDowall.

HOW TO MURDER YOUR WIFE (1965) UA. Screenplay by George Axelrod. Directed by Richard Quine. Starring Jack Lemmon, Virna Lisi, Terry-Thomas.

HUD (1963) Par. Screenplay by Irving Ravetch and Harriet Frank, Jr. Directed by Martin Ritt. Starring Paul Newman, Melvyn Douglas, Patricia Neal, Brandon de Wilde.

HUMORESQUE (1947) WB. Screenplay by Clifford Odets, Zachary Gold, from the novel by Fannie Hurst. Directed by Jean Negulesco. Starring Joan Crawford, John Garfield, Oscar Levant.

HUSTLER, THE (1961) 20th. Screenplay by Robert

Rossen, Sidney Carroll, from the novel by Walter Tevis. Directed by Robert Rossen. Starring Paul Newman, Piper Laurie, George C. Scott, Jackie Gleason.

I AM A FUGITIVE FROM A CHAIN GANG (1932) WB. Screenplay by Howard Green and Beverly Holmes. Directed by Mervyn Leroy. Starring Paul Muni, Glenda Farrell.

I WAS A MALE WAR BRIDE (1949) 20th. Screenplay by Charles Lederer and Leonard Spiegelgass. Directed by Howard Hawks. Starring Cary Grant and Ann Sheridan.

I REMEMBER MAMA (1948) RKO. Screenplay by De Witt Bodeen. Based on the play by John Van Druten and the novel by Kathryn Forbes. Directed by George Stevens. Starring Irene Dunne, Barbara Bel Geddes.

I NEVER SANG FOR MY FATHER (1969) Col. Screenplay by Robert Anderson, from his play. Directed by Gilbert Cates. Starring Melvyn Douglas, Gene Hackman.

I WAS A TEENAGE FRANKENSTEIN (1957) AIP. Screenplay by Kenneth Langtry. Directed by Herbert Strack. Starring Whit Bissell, Phyllis Coates.

THE ICEMAN COMETH (1973) American Film Theatre. Written by Eugene O'Neill. Directed by John Frankenheimer. Starring Lee Marvin, Fredric March, Robert Ryan, Jeff Bridges.

I'M NO ANGEL (1933) Par. Screenplay by Harlan Thompson and Mae West. Directed by Wesley Ruggles. Starring Mae West, Cary Grant, Edward Arnold.

INHERIT THE WIND (1960) UA. Screenplay by Nathan Douglas, Harold Smith. Based on the play by Jerome Lawrence and Robert E. Lee. Directed by Stanley Kramer. Starring Spencer Tracy, Fredric March, Gene Kelly, Dick York.

IN THE HEAT OF THE NIGHT (1967) UA. Screenplay by Stirling Silliphant. Based on the novel by John Ball. Directed by Norman Jewison. Starring Sidney Poitier, Rod Steiger, Lee Grant.

INDISCREET (1958) WB. Screenplay by Norman Krasna, based on his play. Directed by Stanley Donen. Starring Cary Grant and Ingrid Bergman.

INVASION OF THE BODY SNATCHERS (1956) AA. Screenplay by Daniel Mainwaring, from the novel by Jack Finney. Directed by Don Siegel. Starring Kevin McCarthy and Dana Wynter.

INVISIBLE MAN, THE (1933) Univ. Screenplay by R.C. Sheriff, Philip Wylie, from the novel by H.G. Wells. Directed by James Whale. Starring Claude Rains.

ISADORA (1968) Univ. Screenplay by Melvyn Bragg, Clive Exton. Directed by Karel Reisz. Starring Vanessa Redgrave, Jason Robards.

IT HAPPENED ONE NIGHT (1934) Col. Screenplay by Robert Riskin. Based on a story by Samuel Hopkins Adams. Directed by Frank Capra. Starring Clark Gable and Caudette Colbert.

IT'S A WONDERFUL LIFE (1946) RKO. Screenplay by Frances Goodrich, Albert Hackett, Frank Capra. Based on a story by Philip Van Doren Stern. Directed by Frank Capra. Starring James Stewart, Donna Reed, Lionel Barrymore.

JANE EYRE (1943) 20th. Screenplay by Aldous Huxley, Robert Stevenson, John Houseman. Directed by Robert Stevenson. Starring Joan Fontaine, Orson Welles.

JAWS (1975) Univ. Screenplay by Peter Benchley, Carl Gottlieb, Howard Sackler. Based on the novel by Peter Benchley. Directed by Steven Spielberg. Starring Roy Scheider, Robert Shaw, Richard Dreyfuss.

JAZZ SINGER, THE (1927) WB. From the play by

Samson Raphaelson. Directed by Alan Crosland. Starring Al Jolson, Warner Oland.

JESSE JAMES (1939) 20th. Screenplay by Nunnally Johnson. Directed by Henry King. Starring Tyrone Power, Henry Fonda, Nancy Kelly.

JEZEBEL (1938) WB. Screenplay by Clements Ripley, Abem Finkel, John Huston, from the play by Owen Davis. Directed by William Wyler. Starring Bette Davis and Henry Fonda.

JOE (1970) Cannon. Screenplay by Norman Wexler. Directed by John Avildsen. Starring Peter Boyle, Susan Sarandon.

JUDGMENT AT NUREMBERG (1961) UA. Screenplay by Abby Mann. Directed by Stanley Kramer. Starring Spencer Tracy, Burt Lancaster, Richard Widmark, Marlene Dietrich, Maximilian Schell, Judy Garland.

JULIA (1977) 20th. Screenplay by Alvin Sargent. Based on the story by Lillian Hellman. Directed by Fred Zinnemann. Starring Jane Fonda, Vanessa Redgrave, Jason Robards, Maximilian Schell.

JUNE BRIDE (1948) WB. Screenplay by Ranald MacDougall, from the play by Eileen Tighe, Graeme Lorimer. Starring Bette Davis, Robert Montgomery, Fay Bainter.

KEY LARGO (1948) WB. Screenplay by Richard Brooks. Based on the play by Maxwell Anderson. Directed by John Huston. Starring Humphrey Bogart, Lauren Bacall, Edward G. Robinson, Lionel Barrymore.

KING AND I, THE (1956) 20th. Screenplay by Ernest Lehman. Based on the musical by Richard Rodgers and Oscar Hammerstein II, and the book by Margaret Landon. Directed by Walter Lang. Starring Yul Brynner and Deborah Kerr.

KING IN NEW YORK, A (1957) Attica. Written and

directed by Charles Chaplin. Starring Charles Chaplin, Dawn Addams, Michael Chaplin.

KING KONG (1933) RKO. Screenplay by James Crielman, Ruth Rose. Directed by Merian Cooper. Starring Fay Wray, Bruce Cabot, Robert Armstrong.

KINGS ROW (1941) WB. Screenplay by Casey Robinson. Based on the novel by Henry Bellamann. Directed by Sam Wood. Starring Ann Sheridan, Robert Cummings, Ronald Reagan.

KING OF THE MOUNTAIN (1981) Univ. Screenplay by H.R. Christian. Directed by Noel Nosseck. Starring Harry Hamlin, Joseph Bottoms, Dennis Hopper.

KISS OF DEATH (1947) 20th. Screenplay by Ben Hecht, Charles Lederer. Directed by Henry Hathaway. Starring Victor Mature, Richard Widmark, Brian Donleavy.

KITTEN WITH A WHIP (1964) Univ. Written and directed by Douglas Heyes. Based on the book by Wade Miller. Starring Ann-Margret, John Forsythe.

KLONDIKE ANNIE (1936) Par. Screenplay by Mae West, Marion Morgan, George Dowell. Directed by Raoul Walsh. Starring Mae West, Victor McLaglen, Philip Reed.

KLUTE (1971) WB. Screenplay by Andy and Dave Lewis. Directed by Alan Pakula. Starring Jane Fonda and Donald Sutherland.

KNUTE ROCKNE—ALL AMERICAN (1940) WB. Screenplay by Robert Buckner. Directed by Lloyd Bacon. Starring Pat O'Brien, Ronald Reagan.

KRAMER VS. KRAMER (1979) Col. Screenplay and directed by Robert Benton, from the novel by Avery Corman. Starring Dustin Hoffman and Meryl Streep.

LADIES OF LEISURE (1930) Col. Screenplay by Milton Gropper, Jo Swerling. Directed by Frank Capra. Starring Barbara Stanwyck.

LADY EVE, THE (1941) Par. Screenplay and directed by Preston Sturges. Starring Barbara Stanwyck and Henry Fonda.

LAST EMPEROR, THE (1988) Col. Screenplay by Mark Peploe and Bernardo Bertolucci. Directed by Bernardo Bertolucci. Starring Peter O'Toole, John Lone, Joan Chen.

LAST FLIGHT, THE (1931) WB. Screenplay by John Saunders, based on his novel. Directed by William Dieterle. Starring Richard Barthelmess, Helen Chandler.

LAST OF SHEILA, THE (1973) WB. Screenplay by Stephen Sondheim and Anthony Perkins. Directed by Herbert Ross. Starring Richard Benjamin, Dyan Cannon, James Coburn, James Mason.

LAURA (1944) 20th. Screenplay by Jay Dratler, from the novel by Vera Caspary. Directed by Otto Preminger. Starring Gene Tierney, Dana Andrews, Clifton Webb, Vincent Price.

LAWRENCE OF ARABIA (1962) Col. Screenplay by Robert Bolt. Directed by David Lean. Starring Peter O'Toole, Alec Guinness, Anthony Quinn, Jack Hawkins, Claude Rains.

LEGEND OF THE LONE RANGER, THE (1981) ITC. Screenplay by Ivan Goff, Ben Roberts. Directed by William Fraker. Starring Klinton Spilsbury, Michael Horse.

LETTER, THE (1940) WB. Screenplay by Howard Koch, from the story by W. Somerset Maugham. Directed by William Wyler. Starring Bette Davis, Herbert Marshall.

LETTER TO THREE WIVES, A (1948) 20th. Screenplay by Joseph Mankiewicz, from the novel by John Klempner. Directed by Joseph Mankiewicz. Starring Jeanne Crain, Linda Darnell, Ann Sothern, Kirk Douglas, Paul Douglas.

LIFEBOAT (1944) 20th. Screenplay by Jo Swerling.

Directed by Alfred Hitchcock. Starring Tallulah Bankhead, William Bendix, Walter Slezak, Hume Cronyn, John Hodiak.

LIFE WITH FATHER (1947) WB. Screenplay by Donald Ogden Stewart. Based on the play by Howard Lindsay and Russell Crouse. Directed by Michael Curtiz. Starring William Powell, Irene Dunne, Elizabeth Taylor.

LIMELIGHT (1952) UA. Screenplay and directed by Charles Chaplin. Starring Charles Chaplin, Claire Bloom, Sydney Chaplin.

LION IN WINTER, THE (1968) Embassy. Screenplay by James Goldman, based on his play. Directed by Anthony Harvey. Starring Peter O'Toole, Katharine Hepburn.

LITTLE BIG MAN (1970) National General. Screenplay by Calder Willingham, from the novel by Thomas Berger. Directed by Arthur Penn. Starring Dustin Hoffman, Faye Dunaway, Martin Balsam.

LITTLE FOXES, THE (1941) RKO. Screenplay by Lillian Hellman, based on her play. Directed by William Wyler. Starring Bette Davis, Herbert Marshall, Teresa Wright, Dan Duryea, Charles Dingle.

LITTLE SHOP OF HORRORS (1987) WB. Screenplay by Howard Ashman, based on his musical play. Directed by Frank Oz. Starring Rick Moranis, Ellen Greene, Vincent Gardenia, Steve Martin.

LITTLE TOKYO USA (1942) TCF. Screenplay by George Bricker. Directed by Otto Brower. Starring Preston Foster, Brenda Joyce.

LIVES OF THE BENGAL LANCERS (1935) Par. Screenplay by Waldemar Young, John Balderston, Archmed Abdullah, Grover Jones, William McNutt. Directed by Henry Hathaway. Starring Gary Cooper, Franchot Tone, C. Aubrey Smith.

LONELY ARE THE BRAVE (1962) Univ. Screenplay by Dalton Trumbo, from the novel by Edward Abbey. Directed by David Miller. Starring Kirk Douglas, Walter Matthau, Carroll O'Connor.

LONGEST DAY, THE (1962) 20th. Screenplay by Cornelius Ryan, based on his book. Directed by Andrew Morton and Ken Annakin. Starring John Wayne, Robert Mitchum, Henry Fonda, Robert Ryan, Rod Steiger, Robert Wagner.

LONG, HOT SUMMER, THE (1958) 20th. Screenplay by Irving Ravetch and Harriet Frank, Jr. Based on the novel by William Faulkner. Directed by Martin Ritt. Starring Paul Newman, Joanne Woodward, Orson Welles.

LORD LOVE A DUCK (1966) UA. Screenplay by Larry H. Johnson, George Axelrod, from the novel by Al Hine. Directed by George Axelrod. Starring Roddy McDowall, Tuesday Weld, Ruth Gordon.

LOST HORIZON (1937) Col. Screenplay by Robert Riskin. Based on the novel by James Hilton. Directed by Frank Capra. Starring Ronald Colman, Jane Wyatt, Thomas Mitchell.

LOST WEEKEND, THE (1945) Par. Screenplay by Charles Brackett, Billy Wilder. Directed by Billy Wilder. Starring Ray Milland and Jane Wyman.

LOVE AFFAIR (1939) RKO. Screenplay by Delmer Daves and Donald Ogden Stewart. Directed by Leo McCarey. Starring Irene Dunne and Charles Boyer.

LOVE AND DEATH (1975) UA. Screenplay and directed by Woody Allen. Starring Woody Allen, Diane Keaton.

LOVE AT FIRST BITE (1979) Melvin Simon. Screenplay by Robert Kaufman. Directed by Stan Dragote. Starring George Hamilton, Susan St. James, Richard Benjamin.

LOVE FINDS ANDY HARDY (1938) MGM.
Screenplay by William Ludwig. Directed by George Seitz.
Starring Mickey Rooney, Lewis Stone, Judy Garland.

LOVE IS A MANY-SPLENDORED THING (1955)
20th. Screenplay by John Patrick. Directed by Henry King.
Starring William Holden and Jennifer Jones.

LOVE ME TONIGHT (1932) Par. Screenplay by
Samuel Hoffenstein. Directed by Rouben Mamoulian.
Starring Maurice Chevalier, Jeanette MacDonald.

LOVERS AND OTHER STRANGERS (1970) ABC
Pictures. Screenplay by Renee Taylor, Joe Bologna, David
Selag Goodman. Directed by Cy Howard. Starring Gig
Young, Anne Jackson, Bea Arthur, Bob Dishy.

LOVE STORY (1975) Par. Screenplay by Erich
Segal, based on his novel. Directed by Arthur Hiller. Starring Ryan O'Neal, Ali McGraw, Ray Milland.

MACOMBER AFFAIR, THE (1947) UA. Screen-
play by Casey Robinson. Based on the story by Ernest
Hemingway. Directed by Zoltan Korda. Starring Gregory
Peck, Joan Bennett, Robert Preston.

MAGNIFICENT SEVEN, THE (1960) MGM.
Screenplay by William Roberts. Directed by John Sturges.
Starring Yul Brynner, Steve McQueen, Eli Wallach.

MAGNUM FORCE (1973) WB. Screenplay by John
Milius and Michael Cimino. Directed by Ted Post. Starring
Clint Eastwood, Hal Holbrook.

MAJOR AND THE MINOR, THE (1942) Par.
Screenplay by Charles Brackett and Billy Wilder. Directed
by Billy Wilder. Starring Ginger Rogers, Ray Milland,
Robert Benchley.

MAJOR BARBARA (1941) Gabriel Pascal. Screenplay by Anatole Grunwald, Gabriel Pascal. Based on the
play by Bernard Shaw. Directed by Gabriel Pascal. Starring Wendy Hiller, Rex Harrison, Robert Morley.

MALTESE FALCON, THE (1941) WB. Screenplay by John Huston. Based on the novel by Dashiell Hammett. Directed by John Huston. Starring Humphrey Bogart, Mary Astor, Peter Lorre, Sydney Greenstreet, Elisha Cook, Jr.

MAME (1974) WB. Screenplay by Paul Zindel. Based on the play by Jerome Lawrence and Robert E. Lee, and the book by Patrick Dennis. Directed by Gene Saks. Starring Lucille Ball, Bea Arthur, Robert Preston.

MAN AND A WOMAN, A (1966) Leo Films. Screenplay by Claude Lelouch, Pierre Uytterhoven. Directed by Claude Lelouch. Starring Anouk Aimee, Jean-Louis Trintignant.

MAN FOR ALL SEASONS, A (1966) Col. Screenplay by Robert Bolt, based on his play. Directed by Fred Zinnemann. Starring Paul Scofield, Wendy Hiller.

MANHATTAN (1979) UA. Screenplay by Woody Allen and Marshall Brickman. Directed by Woody Allen. Starring Woody Allen, Diane Keaton, Mariel Hemingway, Meryl Streep.

MAN WHO CAME TO DINNER, THE (1941) WB. Screenplay by Julius and Philip Epstein, from the play by George S. Kaufman and Moss Hart. Directed by William Keighley. Starring Monty Woolley, Bette Davis, Ann Sheridan.

MAN WHO SHOT LIBERTY VALANCE, THE (1962) Par. Screenplay by James Bellah, Willis Goldbeck. Directed by John Ford. Starring James Stewart, John Wayne.

MARRIED TO THE MOB (1989) Ori. Screenplay by Barry Strugatz, Mark Burns. Directed by Jonathan Demme. Starring Michelle Pfeiffer, Alec Baldwin.

MARRYING MAN, THE (1991) Hollywood Pictures. Screenplay by Neil Simon. Directed by Jerry Rees. Starring Alec Baldwin and Kim Basinger.

MARTY (1955) UA. Screenplay by Paddy Chayefsky, based on his television play. Directed by Delbert Mann. Starring Ernest Borgnine and Betsy Blair.

MASK OF DIMITRIOS, THE (1944) WB. Screenplay by Frank Gruber, from the novel by Eric Ambler. Directed by Jean Negulesco. Starring Peter Lorre, Zachary Scott.

MATA HARI (1931) MGM. Screenplay by Doris Anderson, Gilbert Emery. Directed by George Fitzmaurice. Starring Greta Garbo, Ramon Novarro, Lionel Barrymore.

MATCHMAKER, THE (1958) Par. Screenplay by John Michael Hayes, from the play by Thornton Wilder. Directed by Joseph Anthony. Starring Shirley Booth, Paul Ford.

MATING SEASON, THE (1951) Par. Screenplay by Walter Reisch, Charles Brackett, Richard Breen. Directed by Mitchell Leisen. Starring Gene Tierney, John Lund.

MEDIUM COOL (1969) Par. Screenplay and directed by Haskell Wexler. Starring Robert Forster, Verna Bloom, Peter Bonerz.

MEET JOHN DOE (1941) WB. Screenplay by Robert Riskin, from a story by Richard Connell and Robert Presnell. Directed by Frank Capra. Starring Gary Cooper, Barbara Stanwyck, Edward Arnold, Walter Brennan.

MELVIN AND HOWARD (1980) Univ. Screenplay by Bo Goldman. Directed by Jonathan Demme. Starring Jason Robards, Paul Le Mat.

MEN, THE (1950) UA. Screenplay by Carl Foreman. Directed by Fred Zinnemann. Starring Marlon Brando, Teresa Wright, Everett Sloane, Jack Webb.

MIDNIGHT (1939) Par. Screenplay by Billy Wilder and Charles Brackett. Directed by Mitchell Leisen. Starring Claudette Colbert, Don Ameche, John Barrymore.

MIDNIGHT COWBOY (1969) UA. Screenplay by Waldo Salt, from the novel by James Leo Herlihy. Directed by John Schlesinger. Starring Dustin Hoffman and Jon Voight.

MILDRED PIERCE (1945) WB. Screenplay by Ranald MacDougall and Catherine Turney. Directed by Michael Curtiz. Starring Joan Crawford, Zachary Scott, Ann Blyth.

MIRACLE OF MORGAN'S CREEK, THE (1944) Par. Screenplay and directed by Preston Sturges. Starring Eddie Bracken and Betty Hutton.

MIRACLE ON 34TH STREET (1947) 20th. Screenplay and directed by George Seaton. Starring Maureen O'Hara, John Payne, Edmund Gwenn, Natalie Wood.

MIRACLE WORKER, THE (1962) UA. Screenplay by William Gibson, based on his play. Directed by Arthur Penn. Starring Anne Bancroft and Patty Duke.

MISFITS, THE (1961) UA. Screenplay by Arthur Miller. Directed by John Huston. Starring Clark Gable, Marilyn Monroe, Montgomery Clift.

MISTER ROBERTS (1955) WB. Screenplay by Frank Nugent, Joshua Logan. Based on the play and novel by Thomas Heggen. Directed by John Ford and Mervyn Leroy. Starring Henry Fonda, James Cagney, Jack Lemmon, William Powell.

MOBY DICK (1956) WB. Screenplay by Ray Bradbury and John Huston, based on the novel by Herman Melville. Directed by John Huston. Starring Gregory Peck, Orson Welles, Richard Basehart.

MOMMIE DEAREST (1982) Par. Screenplay by Frank Yablans, Trace Hotchner, Robert Getchell, from the book by Christina Crawford. Directed by Frank Perry. Starring Faye Dunaway, Steve Forrest.

MONKEY BUSINESS (1931) Par. Screenplay by S.J. Perelman and Will B. Johnstone. Directed by Norman McLeod. Starring Groucho, Chico, Harpo, Zeppo Marx, Thelma Todd.

MONSIEUR VERDOUX (1947) UA. Screenplay and directed by Charles Chaplin. Starring Charles Chaplin and Martha Raye.

MOON IS BLUE, THE (1953) UA. Screenplay by F. Hugh Herbert, based on his play. Directed by Otto Preminger. Starring William Holden, David Niven, Maggie McNamara.

MORE THE MERRIER, THE (1943) Col. Screenplay by Robert Russell, Frank Ross, Richard Flournoy, Lewis Foster. Directed by George Stevens. Starring Jean Arthur, Joel McCrea.

MOULIN ROUGE (1952) UA. Screenplay by Anthony Veiller and John Huston, from the novel by Pierre La Mure. Directed by John Huston. Starring Jose Ferrer and Zsa Zsa Gabor.

MR. BLANDINGS BUILDS HIS DREAM HOUSE (1948) RKO. Screenplay by Norman Panama and Melvin Frank. Based on the novel by Eric Hodgins. Directed by H.C. Potter. Starring Cary Grant, Myrna Loy, Melvyn Douglas.

MR. DEEDS GOES TO TOWN (1936) Col. Screenplay by Clarence Budington Kelland. Directed by Frank Capra. Starring Gary Cooper, Jean Arthur, Lionel Stander.

MR. SKEFFINGTON (1944) WB. Screenplay by Philip and Julius Epstein. Directed by Vincent Sherman. Starring Bette Davis, Claude Rains, Walter Abel.

MR. SMITH GOES TO WASHINGTON (1939) Col.

Screenplay by Sidney Buchman. Directed by Frank Capra. Starring James Stewart, Jean Arthur, Edward Arnold, Claude Rains.

MRS. MINIVER (1942) MGM. Screenplay by Arthur Wimperis. Directed by William Wyler. Starring Greer Garson, Walter Pidgeon, Teresa Wright.

MURDER BY DEATH (1976) Col. Screenplay by Neil Simon. Directed by Robert Moore. Starring David Niven, Maggie Smith, Alec Guinness, Peter Sellers, Peter Falk, Eileen Brennan, James Coco, Truman Capote.

MURDER, MY SWEET (1944) Screenplay by John Paxton, from the novel by Raymond Chandler. Directed by Edward Dmytryk. Starring Dick Powell, Claire Trevor, Mike Mazurki, Anne Shirley.

MUTINY ON THE BOUNTY (1935) MGM. Based on the novel by Charles Nordhoff and James Norman Hall. Directed by Frank Lloyd. Starring Clark Gable, Charles Laughton, Franchot Tone.

MY DINNER WITH ANDRE (1982) Andre Productions. Screenplay by Wallace Shawn and Andre Gregory. Directed by Louis Malle. Starring Wallace Shawn and Andre Gregory.

MY FAIR LADY (1964) WB. Screenplay by Alan Jay Lerner, based on his musical play. Directed by George Cukor. Starring Rex Harrison, Audrey Hepburn, Stanley Holloway, Wilfred Hyde-White.

MY FAVORITE YEAR (1983) MGM/UA. Screenplay by Norman Steinberg, Dennis Palumbo. Directed by Richard Benjamin. Starring Peter O'Toole, Mark Linn-Baker, Joseph Bologna, Bill Macy.

MY MAN GODFREY (1936) Univ. Screenplay by Morrie Ryskind, Eric Hatch, Gregory La Cava. Directed by Gregory La Cava. Starring William Powell, Carole Lombard, Eugene Pallette.

NATURAL, THE (1985) Tri. Screenplay by Roger Towne and Phil Dusenberry from the novel by Bernard Malamud. Directed by Barry Levinson. Starring Robert Redford, Robert Duvall, Glenn Close, Kim Basinger.

NETWORK (1976) UA. Screenplay by Paddy Chayefsky. Directed by Sidney Lumet. Starring Faye Dunaway, William Holden, Peter Finch, Robert Duvall, Ned Beatty.

NEVER GIVE A SUCKER AN EVEN BREAK (1941) Screenplay by John Neville, Prescott Chaplin. Directed by Edward Clive. Starring W.C. Fields, Gloria Jean, Franklin Pangborn, Margaret Dumont.

NIGHT AFTER NIGHT (1932) Par. Screenplay by Vincent Laurence, from the novel by Louis Bromfield. Directed by Archie Mayo. Starring George Raft, Mae West.

NIGHT AT THE OPERA, A (1935) MGM. Screenplay by George S. Kaufman, Morrie Ryskind. Directed by Sam Wood. Starring Groucho, Chico, Harpo Marx, Kitty Carlisle, Allan Jones.

NIGHT IN CASABLANCA, A (1946) David L. Loew. Screenplay by Joseph Fields, Roland Kibbee, Frank Tashlin. Directed by Archie Mayo. Starring Groucho, Chico, Harpo Marx, Sig Rumann.

NIGHT OF THE IGUANA, THE (1964) MGM. Screenplay by Anthony Veiller. Based on the play by Tennessee Williams. Directed by John Huston. Starring Richard Burton, Ava Gardner, Deborah Kerr, Sue Lyon.

NINOTCHKA (1939) MGM. Screenplay by Charles Brackett, Billy Wilder, Walter Reisch. Directed by Ernst Lubitsch. Starring Greta Garbo and Melvyn Douglas.

NONE BUT THE LONELY HEART (1944) RKO. Screenplay by Clifford Odets. Based on the novel by Richard Llewellyn. Directed by Clifford Odets. Starring Cary Grant, Ethel Barrymore, Barry Fitzgerald.

NORTH BY NORTHWEST (1959) MGM. Screenplay by Ernest Lehman. Directed by Alfred Hitchcock. Starring Cary Grant, Eva Marie Saint, James Mason, Leo G. Carroll.

NOTHING IN COMMON (1986) Tri. Screenplay by Rick Podell and Michael Preminger. Directed by Garry Marshall. Starring Jackie Gleason and Tom Hanks.

NOTHING SACRED (1937) UA. Screenplay by Ben Hecht, from a story by James Street. Directed by William Wellman. Starring Carole Lombard, Fredric March.

NOTORIOUS (1946) RKO. Screenplay by Ben Hecht. Directed by Alfred Hitchcock. Starring Cary Grant, Ingrid Bergman, Claude Rains, Louis Calhern.

NOW, VOYAGER (1942) WB. Screenplay by Casey Robinson, from the novel by Olive Higgins Prouty. Directed by Irving Rapper. Starring Bette Davis, Paul Henreid, Claude Rains.

OBJECTIVE BURMA (1944) WB. Screenplay by Ranald MacDougall, Lester Cole, Alvah Bessie. Directed by Raoul Walsh. Starring Errol Flynn, William Prince.

ODD COUPLE, THE (1968) Par. Screenplay by Neil Simon, based on his play. Directed by Gene Saks. Starring Jack Lemmon and Walter Matthau.

OH, GOD! (1977) Screenplay by Larry Gelbart, from the novel by Avery Corman. Directed by Carl Reiner. Starring George Burns, John Denver, Teri Garr.

OH! WHAT A LOVELY WAR (1969) Par. Screenplay by Len Deighton. Directed by Richard Attenborough. Starring Richard Attenborough, Ralph Richardson, John Gielgud, Kenneth More.

OKLAHOMA! (1955) Magna. Screenplay by Sonya Levien and William Ludwig, from the musical by Richard Rodgers and Oscar Hammerstein II. Directed by Fred Zinnemann. Starring Gordon MacRae, Shirley Jones, Gloria Grahame, Charlotte Greenwood, Rod Steiger.

OLD MAN AND THE SEA, THE (1958) WB. Screenplay by Peter Viertel, from the novel by Ernest Hemingway. Starring Spencer Tracy.

ON THE WATERFRONT (1954) Col. Screenplay by Budd Schulberg. Directed by Elia Kazan. Starring Marlon Brando, Karl Malden, Lee J. Cobb, Rod Steiger, Eva Marie Saint.

ON GOLDEN POND (1982) Marble Arch Productions. Screenplay by Ernest Thompson, from his play. Directed by Mark Rydell. Starring Henry Fonda, Katharine Hepburn, Jane Fonda, Dabney Coleman.

ONE-EYED JACKS (1961) Par. Screenplay by Guy Trosper, Calder Willingham, from the novel by Charles Neider. Directed by Marlon Brando. Starring Marlon Brando, Karl Malden, Katy Jurado.

ONE, TWO, THREE (1961) UA. Screenplay by Billy Wilder, I.A.L. Diamond, from the play by Ferenc Molnar. Directed by Billy Wilder. Starring James Cagney, Horst Bucholtz, Arlene Francis.

ONE FLEW OVER THE CUCKOO'S NEST (1975) UA. Screenplay by Lawrence Hauben, Bo Goldman, from the play by Dale Wasserman. Directed by Milos Forman. Starring Jack Nicholson, Louise Fletcher, Scatman Crothers.

ONLY WHEN I LAUGH (1982) Col. Screenplay by Neil Simon. Directed by Glenn Jordan. Starring Marsha Mason, Kristy McNichol, Joan Hackett.

OUTLAND (1982) WB. Screenplay and directed by Peter Hyams. Starring Sean Connery, Peter Boyle, Frances Sternhagen.

OUTLAW JOSIE WALES, THE (1976) WB. Screenplay by Phil Kaufman, Sonia Chernus, from the novel by Forrest Carter. Directed by Clint Eastwood. Starring Clint Eastwood and Sondra Locke.

OUT OF AFRICA (1986) Univ. Screenplay by Kurt Luedtke, from the memoirs of Isak Dinesen. Directed by Sydney Pollack. Starring Meryl Streep, Robert Redford, Klaus Maria Brandauer.

OX-BOW INCIDENT, THE (1943) 20th. Screenplay by Lamar Trotti, from the novel by Walter Van Tilburg Clark. Directed by William Wellman. Starring Henry Fonda, Dana Andrews, Anthony Quinn, Harry Morgan.

PAL JOEY (1957) Col. Screenplay by Dorothy Kingsley, based on the musical play by John O'Hara. Directed by George Sidney. Starring Frank Sinatra, Ava Gardner, Kim Novak.

PALM BEACH STORY, THE (1942) Univ. Screenplay and directed by Preston Sturges. Starring Claudette Colbert, Joel McCrea, Rudy Vallee.

PAPER CHASE, THE (1973) Screenplay by James Bridges, from the novel by John Jay Osborn, Jr. Directed by James Bridges. Starring Timothy Bottoms and John Houseman.

PAT AND MIKE (1952) MGM. Screenplay by Ruth Gordon, Garson Kanin. Directed by George Cukor. Starring Spencer Tracy, Katharine Hepburn, Aldo Ray.

PATTON (1970) 20th. Screenplay by Francis Ford Coppola and Edmund North. Directed by Franklin Schaffner. Starring George C. Scott, Karl Malden.

PEGGY SUE GOT MARRIED (1987) Tri. Screenplay by Jerry Leightling and Arlene Sarner. Directed by Francis Ford Coppola. Starring Kathleen Turner, Nicolas Cage.

PETE KELLY'S BLUES (1955) WB. Screenplay by Richard Breen. Directed by Jack Webb. Starring Jack Webb, Janet Leigh, Edmond O'Brien.

PETE 'N' TILLY (1972) Univ. Screenplay by Julius Epstein, from the novel by Peter de Vries. Directed by Martin Ritt. Starring Walter Matthau, Carol Burnett.

PETRIFIED FOREST, THE (1936) WB. Screenplay by Charles Kenyon, Delmer Daves. Directed by Archie Mayo. Starring Leslie Howard, Bette Davis, Humphrey Bogart.

PHILADELPHIA STORY, THE (1940) MGM. Screenplay by Donald Ogden Stewart, from the play by Philip Barry. Directed by George Cukor. Starring Cary Grant, Katharine Hepburn, James Stewart, Ruth Hussey.

PICNIC (1950) Col. Screenplay by Daniel Taradash. Based on the play by William Inge. Directed by Joshua Logan. Starring William Holden, Rosalind Russell, Kim Novak, Betty Field.

PICTURE OF DORIAN GRAY, THE (1945) MGM. Screenplay by Albert Lewin, from the novel by Oscar Wilde. Directed by Albert Lewis. Starring Hurd Hatfield, George Sanders, Donna Reed, Angela Lansbury.

PILLOW TALK (1959) Univ. Screenplay by Stanley Shapiro, Maurice Richlin. Directed by Michael Gordon. Starring Rock Hudson, Doris Day, Tony Randall.

PINK PANTHER, THE (1964) UA. Screenplay by Maurice Richlin, Blake Edwards. Directed by Blake Edwards. Starring Peter Sellers, David Niven, Robert Wagner, Capucine.

PLACE IN THE SUN, A (1951) Par. Screenplay by Michael Wilson, Harry Brown. Based on the novel by Theodore Dreiser. Directed by George Stevens. Starring Montgomery Clift, Elizabeth Taylor, Shelley Winters.

PLAINSMAN, THE (1936) Par. Screenplay by Waldemar Young, Lynn Riggs, Harold Lamb. Directed by Cecil B. De Mille. Starring Gary Cooper, Jean Arthur, Charles Bickford.

PLATOON (1987) Ori. Screenplay and directed by Oliver Stone. Starring Tom Berenger, Willem Dafoe, Charlie Sheen.

PLAY IT AGAIN, SAM (1972) Par. Screenplay by Woody Allen from his play. Directed by Herbert Ross. Starring Woody Allen, Diane Keaton, Tony Roberts.

PLAY MISTY FOR ME (1971) Univ. Screenplay by Jo Heims, Deain Reisner. Directed by Clint Eastwood. Starring Clint Eastwood and Jessica Walter.

POSEIDON ADVENTURE, THE (1972) 20th. Screenplay by Stirling Silliphant and Wendell Mayes, from the novel by Paul Gallico. Directed by Ronald Neame. Starring Gene Hackman, Ernest Borgnine, Red Buttons, Shelley Winters.

POSSESSED (1947) WB. Screenplay by Silvia Richards. Directed by Curtin Bernhardt. Starring Joan Crawford, Van Heflin, Raymond Massey.

PRIDE AND PREJUDICE (1940) MGM. Screenplay by Aldous Huxley, from the novel by Jane Austen. Directed by Robert Z. Leonard. Starring Laurence Olivier, Greer Garson, Mary Boland, Edmund Gwenn, Maureen O'Sullivan.

PRIDE OF THE MARINES (1945) WB. Screenplay by Albert Maltz. Directed by Delmer Daves. Starring John Garfield, Eleanor Parker, Dane Clark.

PRIDE OF THE YANKEES (1942) RKO. Screenplay by Jo Swerling and Herman Mankiewicz. Directed by John Sherwood. Starring Gary Cooper, Teresa Wright, Babe Ruth.

PRIME OF MISS JEAN BRODIE, THE (1969) 20th. Screenplay by Jay Presson Allen, from her stage adaptation of the novel by Muriel Spark. Directed by Ronald Neame. Starring Maggie Smith, Pamela Franklin.

PRINCESS BRIDE, THE (1988) 20th. Screenplay by William Goldman, based on his novel. Directed by Rob Reiner. Starring Mandy Patinkin, Chris Sarandon, Wallace Shawn.

PRIVATE BENJAMIN (1980) WB. Screenplay by

Nancy Meyers, Charles Shyer, Harvey Miller. Directed by Howard Zieff. Starring Goldie Hawn, Eileen Brennan.

PRIVATE LIFE OF HENRY VIII, THE (1933) UA. Screenplay by Lajos Boro and Arthur Wimperis. Directed by Alexander Korda. Starring Charles Laughton, Merle Oberon, Wendy Barrie, Elsa Lanchester.

PRIVATE LIVES (1931) MGM. Screenplay by Hans Kraly, Claudine West, Richard Schayer, from the play by Noel Coward. Directed by Hans Kraly. Starring Norma Shearer, Robert Montgomery.

PRIZZI'S HONOR (1986) 20th. Screenplay by Richard Condon and Janet Roach, from the novel by Richard Condon. Directed by John Huston. Starring Jack Nicholson, Kathleen Turner, Anjelica Huston.

PRODUCERS, THE (1968) Embassy. Written and directed by Mel Brooks. Starring Zero Mostel, Gene Wilder, Dick Shawn, Kenneth Mars.

PSYCHO (1960) Par. Screenplay by Joseph Stefano, from the novel by Robert Bloch. Directed by Alfred Hitchcock. Starring Anthony Perkins, Janet Leigh, Vera Miles, Martin Balsam.

PUNCHLINE (1989) Col. Written and directed by David Seltzer. Starring Tom Hanks and Sally Field.

PYGMALION (1938) MGM. Screenplay by Bernard Shaw, from his play. Directed by Anthony Asquith and Leslie Howard. Starring Leslie Howard, Wendy Hiller.

QUIET MAN, THE (1952) Rep. Screenplay by Frank Nugent. Directed by John Ford. Starring John Wayne, Maureen O'Hara, Victor McLaglen.

QUO VADIS (1951) MGM. Screenplay by John Lee Mahon, S.N. Behrman, Sonya Levien, from the novel by Henryk Sienkiewicz. Directed by Mervyn Leroy. Starring Robert Taylor, Deborah Kerr, Leo Genn, Peter Ustinov.

RADIO DAYS (1988) Ori. Screenplay and directed

by Woody Allen. Starring Woody Allen, Mia Farrow, Dianne Wiest, Josh Mostel, Wallace Shawn.

RAIDERS OF THE LOST ARK (1981) Par. Screenplay by Lawrence Kasdan. Directed by Steven Spielberg. Starring Harrison Ford, Karen Allen.

RAIN PEOPLE, THE (1969) WB. Screenplay and directed by Francis Ford Coppola. Starring James Caan, Robert Duvall, Shirley Knight.

RAISING ARIZONA (1988) 20th. Screenplay by Ethan and Joel Coen. Directed by Joel Coen. Starring Nicolas Cage, Holly Hunter, John Goodman.

RAMBO: FIRST BLOOD, PART II (1986) Tri. Screenplay by Sylvester Stallone and James Cameron. Directed by George Cosmatos. Starring Sylvester Stallone, Richard Crenna.

RAMBO III (1989) Tri. Screenplay by Sylvester Stallone and Sheldon Lettich. Directed by Peter MacDonald. Starring Sylvester Stallone, Richard Crenna.

RAZOR'S EDGE, THE (1946) 20th. Screenplay by Lamar Trotti, from the novel by W. Somerset Maugham. Directed by Edmund Goulding. Starring Tyrone Power, Gene Tierney, John Payne, Anne Baxter.

REAR WINDOW (1954) Par. Screenplay by John Michael Hayes. Directed by Alfred Hitchcock. Starring James Stewart, Grace Kelly, Thelma Ritter, Raymond Burr.

REBECCA (1940) UA. Screenplay by Robert E. Sherwood and Joan Harrison. Directed by Alfred Hitchcock. Starring Laurence Olivier, Joan Fontaine, George Sanders, Judith Anderson.

REBEL WITHOUT A CAUSE (1955) WB. Screenplay by Stewart Stern. Directed by Nicholas Ray. Starring James Dean, Natalie Wood, Sal Mineo.

REFLECTIONS IN A GOLDEN EYE (1967) WB.

Screenplay by Chapman Mortimer, Gladys Hill, from the novel by Carson McCullers. Starring Marlon Brando, Elizabeth Taylor, Julie Harris.

REVOLUTION (1985) WB. Screenplay by Robert Dillon. Directed by Hugh Hudson. Starring Al Pacino.

RICH AND FAMOUS (1982) MGM/UA. Screenplay by Gerald Ayres, from the play by John van Druten. Directed by George Cukor. Starring Jacqueline Bisset, Candice Bergen.

RICHARD'S THINGS (1982) New World Pictures. Screenplay by Frederic Raphael, based on his novel. Directed by Anthony Harvey. Starring Liv Ullmann, Amanda Redman.

RICHARD III (1955) London Films. Written by William Shakespeare. Adapted by Laurence Olivier, Alan Dent. Directed by Laurence Olivier. Starring Laurence Olivier, Claire Bloom, Ralph Richardson, Cedric Hardwicke.

ROAD TO BALI (1952) Par. Screenplay by Frank Butler, Hal Kanter, William Morrow. Directed by Hal Walker. Starring Bing Crosby, Bob Hope, Dorothy Lamour.

ROAD TO MOROCCO (1942) Par. Screenplay by Frank Butler and Don Hartman. Directed by David Butler. Starring Bing Crosby, Bob Hope, Dorothy Lamour, Anthony Quinn.

ROAD TO RIO (1947) Par. Screenplay by Edmund Beloin and Jack Rose. Directed by Norman Z. McLeod. Starring Bing Crosby, Bob Hope, Dorothy Lamour.

ROARING TWENTIES, THE (1939) WB. Screenplay by Jerry Wald, Richard Macaulay, Robert Rossen. Directed by Raoul Walsh and Anatole Litvak. Starring James Cagney, Priscilla Lane, Humphrey Bogart.

ROBERTA (1935) RKO. Screenplay by Jane Murfin,

Sam Mintz, from the musical by Jerome Kern and Otto Harbach. Starring Irene Dunne, Fred Astaire, Ginger Rogers.

ROCKY (1976) UA. Screenplay by Sylvester Stallone. Directed by John Avildsen. Starring Sylvester Stallone, Talia Shire, Burt Young, Carl Weathers, Burgess Meredith.

ROMAN HOLIDAY (1953) Par. Screenplay by Ian McClellan Hunter and John Dighton. Directed by William Wyler. Starring Gregory Peck, Audrey Hepburn, Eddie Albert.

ROOM AT THE TOP (1959) Continental. Screenplay by Neil Paterson, from the novel by John Braine. Directed by Jack Clayton. Starring Laurence Harvey, Simone Signoret.

ROSE MARIE (1936) MGM. Screenplay by Frances Goodrich and Albert Hackett, Alice Duer Miller. Based on the musical by Otto Harbach and Oscar Hammerstein II. Directed by W.S. Van Dyke. Starring Jeanette MacDonald, Nelson Eddy.

ROSEMARY'S BABY (1968) Par. Screenplay by Roman Polanski, from the novel by Ira Levin. Directed by Roman Polanski. Starring Mia Farrow, John Cassavetes, Ruth Gordon, Sidney Blackmer.

ROSE TATTOO, THE (1955) Par. Screenplay by Tennessee Williams, based on his play. Directed by Daniel Mann. Starring Anna Magnani and Burt Lancaster.

ROSIE THE RIVETER (1944) Rep. Screenplay by Jack Townley and Aileen Leslie. Directed by Joseph Santley. Starring Frank Albertson, Jane Frazee.

RULING CLASS, THE (1972) Embassy. Screenplay by Peter Barnes, based on his play. Directed by Peter Medak. Starring Peter O'Toole, Alastair Sim.

RUSSIANS ARE COMING THE RUSSIANS ARE

COMING, THE (1966) UA. Screenplay by William Rose. Directed by Norman Jewison. Starring Carl Reiner, Eva Marie Saint, Jonathan Winters.

RUTHLESS PEOPLE (1987) Tou. Screenplay by Dale Launer. Directed by Jim Abrahams, David and Jerry Zucker. Starring Bette Midler, Danny DeVito, Judge Reinhold.

SABOTEUR (1942) Univ. Screenplay by Peter Viertel, Joan Harrison, Dorothy Parker. Directed by Alfred Hitchcock. Starring Robert Cummings, Otto Kruger.

SALVADOR (1987) Hemdale. Screenplay by Oliver Stone and Richard Boyle. Directed by Oliver Stone. Starring James Woods, James Belushi, Michael Murphy.

SAME TIME, NEXT YEAR (1978) Univ. Screenplay by Bernard Slade, based on his play. Directed by Robert Mulligan. Starring Alan Alda and Ellen Burstyn.

SAND PEBBLES, THE (1966) 20th. Screenplay by Robert Anderson, from the novel by Richard McKenna. Directed by Robert Wise. Starring Steve McQueen, Richard Attenborough, Candice Bergen.

SAVE THE TIGER (1973) Screenplay by Steve Shagan. Directed by John Avildsen. Starring Jack Lemmon, Jack Gilford.

SAXON CHARM, THE (1948) Univ. Screenplay and directed by Claude Binyon, from the novel by Frederick Wakeman. Starring Robert Montgomery, Susan Hayward.

SAYONARA (1957) WB. Screenplay by Paul Osborn. Directed by Joshua Logan. Starring Marlon Brando, Red Buttons, Ricardo Montalban.

SCARFACE (1984) Univ. Screenplay by Oliver Stone, from the film and the novel by Armitage Trail. Directed by Brian DePalma. Starring Al Pacino, Michelle Pfeiffer, Robert Loggia.

SCOUNDREL, THE (1935) Par. Screenplay and directed by Ben Hecht, Charles MacArthur. Starring Noel Coward, Alexander Woolcott.

SEPARATE TABLES (1958) UA. Screenplay by Terence Rattigan and John Gay, based on the play by Terence Rattigan. Directed by Delbert Mann. Starring Rita Hayworth, Deborah Kerr, David Niven.

SERGEANT YORK (1941) WB. Screenplay by Abem Finkel, Harry Chandler, Howard Koch, John Huston. Directed by Howard Hawks. Starring Gary Cooper, Walter Brennan, Joan Leslie.

SEVEN BRIDES FOR SEVEN BROTHERS (1954) MGM. Screenplay by Albert Hackett and Frances Goodrich, Dorothy Kingsley. Directed by Stanley Donen. Starring Jane Powell, Howard Keel, Russ Tamblyn.

SEVEN YEAR ITCH, THE (1955) 20th. Screenplay by Billy Wilder, George Axelrod, from the play by George Axelrod. Directed by Billy Wilder. Starring Marilyn Monroe, Tom Ewell, Evelyn Keyes.

SHANE (1953) Par. Screenplay by A.B. Guthrie, Jr., from the novel by Jack Shaefer. Directed by George Stevens. Starring Alan Ladd, Jean Arthur, Van Heflin, Brandon de Wilde, Jack Palance.

SHE DONE HIM WRONG (1933) Par. Screenplay by Harvey Thaw and John Bright, from the play by Mae West. Directed by Lowell Sherman. Starring Mae West and Cary Grant.

SHEENA (1985) Col. Screenplay by David Newman, Lorenzo Semple, Jr. Directed by John Guillermin. Starring Tanya Roberts, Ted Wass.

SHE WORE A YELLOW RIBBON (1949) RKO. Screenplay by Frank Nugent, Laurence Stallings. Directed by John Ford. Starring Joanne Dru, John Agar, Ben Johnson.

SHINING, THE (1980) WB. Screenplay by Stanley

Kubrick, Diane Johnson, from the novel by Stephen King. Directed by Stanley Kubrick. Starring Jack Nicholson.

SHIP OF FOOLS (1965) Col. Screenplay by Abby Mann, from the novel by Katherine Anne Porter. Directed by Stanley Kramer. Starring Vivien Leigh, Lee Marvin, Jose Ferrer, Oskar Werner.

SHOP AROUND THE CORNER, THE (1939) MGM. Screenplay by Samson Raphaelson, from the play by Nikolaus Lazzlo. Directed by Ernst Lubitsch. Starring James Stewart, Margaret Sullavan, Frank Morgan.

SILK STOCKINGS (1957) MGM. Screenplay by Leonard Gershe and Leonard Spiegelgass, from the play by George S. Kaufman, Leueen McGrath, Abe Burrows, from the film "Ninotchka." Directed by Rouben Mamoulian. Starring Fred Astaire, Cyd Charisse, Janis Paige.

SILVERADO (1986) Col. Screenplay by Lawrence Kasdan, Mark Kasdan. Directed by Lawrence Kasdan. Starring Kevin Kline, Scott Glenn, Kevin Costner, Danny Glover, Linda Hunt, John Cleese.

SINCE YOU WENT AWAY (1944) UA. Screenplay by David O. Selznick, from the novel by Margaret Buell Wilder. Directed by John Cromwell. Starring Claudette Colbert, Jennifer Jones, Joseph Cotten, Shirley Temple.

SINGIN' IN THE RAIN (1952) MGM. Screenplay by Adolph Green, Betty Comden. Directed by Gene Kelly, Stanley Donen. Starring Gene Kelly, Donald O'Connor, Debbie Reynolds.

SITTING PRETTY (1948) 20th. Screenplay by F. Hugh Herbert, from the novel by Gwen Davenport. Directed by Walter Lang. Starring Clifton Webb, Robert Young, Maureen O'Hara.

SLEUTH (1972) 20th. Screenplay by Anthony Shaffer, based on his play. Directed by Joseph Mankiewicz. Starring Laurence Olivier and Michael Caine.

SOME CAME RUNNING (1958) MGM. Screenplay by John Patrick, from the novel by James Jones. Directed by Vincente Minnelli. Starring Frank Sinatra, Dean Martin, Shirley MacLaine.

SOME LIKE IT HOT (1959) UA. Screenplay by Billy Wilder and I.A.L. Diamond. Directed by Billy Wilder. Starring Marilyn Monroe, Jack Lemmon, Tony Curtis.

SONG OF BERNADETTE, THE (1942) MGM. Screenplay by George Seaton, from the novel by Franz Werfel. Directed by Henry King. Starring Jennifer Jones, Charles Bickford, Vincent Price, William Eythe.

SON OF PALEFACE (1952) Par. Screenplay and directed by Frank Tashlin. Starring Bob Hope, Jane Russell, Roy Rogers.

SONG TO REMEMBER, A (1945) Col. Screenplay by Sidney Buchman. Directed by Charles Vidor. Starring Paul Muni, Merle Oberon, Cornel Wilde.

SOPHIE'S CHOICE (1983) Univ. Screenplay by Alan Pakula, from the novel by William Styron. Directed by Alan Pakula. Starring Meryl Streep, Kevin Kline, Peter MacNicol.

SOUND OF MUSIC, THE (1965) 20th. Screenplay by Ernest Lehman, from the musical by Richard Rodgers and Oscar Hammerstein II. Directed by Robert Wise. Starring Julie Andrews, Christopher Plummer, Eleanor Parker, Richard Haydn.

SPARTACUS (1960) Univ. Screenplay by Dalton Trumbo, from the novel by Howard Fast. Directed by Stanley Kubrick. Starring Kirk Douglas, Laurence Olivier, Tony Curtis, Charles Laughton, Peter Ustinov.

SPELLBOUND (1945) UA. Screenplay by Ben Hecht, from the novel by Francis Beeding. Directed by Alfred Hitchcock. Starring Ingrid Bergman, Gregory Peck, Leo G. Carroll.

SPY WHO CAME IN FROM THE COLD, THE (1965) Par. Screenplay by Paul Dehn and Guy Trosper. Based on the novel by John LeCarré. Directed by Martin Ritt. Starring Richard Burton, Claire Bloom, Oskar Werner.

STAGE DOOR (1937) RKO. Screenplay by Morrie Ryskind, Anthony Veiller, from the play by Edna Ferber and George S. Kaufman. Directed by Gregory La Cava. Starring Katharine Hepburn, Ginger Rogers, Adolphe Menjou.

STAIRWAY TO HEAVEN (1981) Col. Screenplay by A.J. Carothers. Directed by Richard Rush. Starring John Travolta.

STAND BY ME (1986) Col. Screenplay by Raynold Gideon, Bruce Evans, from the novella by Stephen King. Directed by Rob Reiner. Starring River Phoenix.

STARDUST MEMORIES (1980) MGM/UA. Screenplay and directed by Woody Allen. Starring Woody Allen, Charlotte Rampling, Tony Roberts.

STAR IS BORN, A (1954) Screenplay by Moss Hart. Directed by George Cukor. Starring Judy Garland, James Mason, Charles Bickford, Jack Carson.

STAR WARS (1977) 20th. Screenplay and directed by George Lucas. Starring Alec Guinness, Mark Hamill, Harrison Ford, Carrie Fisher.

STATE OF THE UNION (1948) MGM. Screenplay by Anthony Veiller, from the play by Howard Lindsay and Russell Crouse. Directed by Frank Capra. Starring Spencer Tracy, Katharine Hepburn, Van Johnson, Angela Lansbury.

STING, THE (1973) Univ. Screenplay by David Ward. Directed by George Roy Hill. Starring Paul Newman, Robert Redford, Robert Shaw, Charles Durning.

STORY OF G.I. JOE, THE (1945) UA. Screenplay by Leopold Atlas, Guy Endore, Philip Stevenson. Directed by William Wellman. Starring Burgess Meredith, Robert Mitchum.

STRANGERS ON A TRAIN (1951) WB. Screenplay by Raymond Chandler, Czenzi Ormonde. Directed by Alfred Hitchcock. Starring Farley Granger, Robert Walker, Ruth Roman.

STREETCAR NAMED DESIRE, A (1951) WB. Screenplay and directed by Elia Kazan, from the play by Tennessee Williams. Starring Vivien Leigh, Marlon Brando, Kim Hunter, Karl Malden.

STRIPES (1982) Col. Screenplay by Len Blum, Dan Goldberg, Harold Ramis. Directed by Ivan Reitman. Starring Bill Murray, Harold Ramis, Warren Oates, John Candy.

SUBJECT WAS ROSES, THE (1968) MGM. Screenplay by Frank Gilroy, based on his play. Directed by Ulu Grosbard. Starring Patricia Neal, Jack Albertson, Martin Sheen.

SUDDENLY LAST SUMMER (1959) Col. Screenplay by Gore Vidal and Tennessee Williams, from the play by Tennessee Williams. Directed by Joseph Mankiewicz. Starring Katharine Hepburn and Montgomery Clift.

SULLIVAN'S TRAVELS (1941) Par. Screenplay and directed by Preston Sturges. Starring Joel McCrea, Veronica Lake, William Demarest.

SUMMER WISHES, WINTER DREAMS (1973) Col. Screenplay by Stewart Stern. Directed by Gilbert Cates. Starring Joanne Woodward, Martin Balsam.

SUNSET BOULEVARD (1950) Par. Screenplay by Charles Brackett, Billy Wilder, D.M. Marshman. Directed by Billy Wilder. Starring William Holden, Gloria Swanson, Erich Von Stroheim, Nancy Olson.

SUNSHINE BOYS, THE (1975) UA. Screenplay by Neil Simon, from his play. Directed by Herbert Ross.

Starring Walter Matthau, George Burns, Richard Benjamin.

SUPERMAN II. (1980) Screenplay by Mario Puzo, David Newman, Leslie Newman, Robert Benton. Directed by Richard Donner. Starring Christopher Reeve, Gene Hackman, Margot Kidder.

SURRENDER (1931) Fox. Screenplay by S.N. Behrman, Sonya Levien, from the play by Pierre Benard. Directed by William Howard. Starring Warner Baxter.

SWEET BIRD OF YOUTH (1962) MGM. Screenplay by Richard Brooks, from the play by Tennessee Williams. Directed by Richard Brooks. Starring Paul Newman, Geraldine Page, Ed Begley, Rip Torn.

SWEET LIBERTY (1986) Univ. Screenplay and directed by Alan Alda. Starring Alan Alda, Michael Caine, Michelle Pfeiffer, Bob Hoskins.

SWEET SMELL OF SUCCESS (1957) MGM/UA. Screenplay by Clifford Odets and Ernest Lehman. Directed by Alexander Mackendrick. Starring Burt Lancaster and Tony Curtis.

SWING TIME (1936) RKO. Screenplay by Howard Lindsay, Allan Scott. Directed by George Stevens. Starring Fred Astaire, Ginger Rogers, Victor Moore.

TAKE THE MONEY AND RUN (1969) Palomar. Screenplay by Woody Allen and Mickey Rose. Directed by Woody Allen. Starring Woody Allen, Janet Margolin.

TALE OF TWO CITIES, A (1935) MGM. Screenplay by W.P. Lipscomb and S.N. Behrman. Based on the novel by Charles Dickens. Directed by Jack Conway. Starring Ronald Colman, Basil Rathbone, Edna May Oliver.

TALK RADIO (1989) Univ. Screenplay by Eric Bogosian and Oliver Stone, from the play by Eric Bogosian. Directed by Oliver Stone. Starring Eric Bogosian.

TARZAN THE APE MAN (1932) MGM. Screenplay

by Cyril Hume, Ivor Novello, from characters created by Edgar Rice Burroughs. Directed by W.S. Van Dyke. Starring Johnny Weissmuller and Maureen O'Sullivan.

TAXI DRIVER (1976) Col. Screenplay by Paul Shrader. Directed by Martin Scorsese. Starring Robert De Niro, Cybill Shepherd, Jodie Foster.

TEA AND SYMPATHY (1956) MGM. Screenplay by Robert Anderson, based on his play. Directed by Vincente Minnelli. Starring Deborah Kerr, John Kerr.

TEAHOUSE OF THE AUGUST MOON, THE (1956) MGM. Screenplay by John Patrick, from the novel by Vern Sneider and the play by John Patrick. Directed by Daniel Mann. Starring Marlon Brando, Glenn Ford, Eddie Albert.

TEN COMMANDMENTS, THE (1956) Par. Screenplay by Aeneas Mackenzie, Jesse Lasky, Jack Garnes, Fredric Frank. Directed by Cecil B. De Mille. Starring Charlton Heston, Yul Brynner, Anne Baxter, Edward G. Robinson.

TERMS OF ENDEARMENT (1983) Screenplay and directed by James L. Brooks. Starring Shirley MacLaine, Debra Winger, Jack Nicholson, Danny De Vito.

THAT CERTAIN FEELING (1956) Par. Screenplay by Norman Panama, Melvin Frank, from a play by Jean Kerr. Directed by Norman Panama and Melvin Frank. Starring Bob Hope, George Sanders, Eva Marie Saint.

THEY SHOOT HORSES, DON'T THEY? (1969) Cinerama. Screenplay by James Roe and Robert Thompson, from the novel by Horace McCoy. Directed by Sydney Pollack. Starring Jane Fonda, Michael Sarrazin, Red Buttons, Gig Young.

THIEF OF BAGDAD, THE (1940) UA. Screenplay by Miles Malleson. Directed by Ludwig Berger, Tim Whelan, Michael Powell. Starring Sabu, Conrad Veidt.

THINGS CHANGE (1989) Col. Screenplay by David Mamet and Shel Silverstein. Directed by David Mamet. Starring Don Ameche, Joe Mantegna, Robert Prosky.

THIRD MAN, THE (1949) London Films. Screenplay by Graham Greene. Directed by Sir Carol Reed. Starring Orson Welles, Joseph Cotten, Alida Valli.

THIS LAND IS MINE (1943) RKO. Screenplay by Dudley Nichols. Directed by Jean Renoir. Starring Charles Laughton, Maureen O'Hara, George Sanders.

THOUSAND CLOWNS, A (1965) UA. Screenplay by Herb Gardner, based on his play. Directed by Fred Coe. Starring Jason Robards, Barry Gordon, Barbara Harris, Martin Balsam, William Daniels.

THREE COINS IN THE FOUNTAIN (1954) 20th. Screenplay by John Patrick. Directed by Jean Negulesco. Starring Clifton Webb, Dorothy McGuire, Jean Peters, Louis Jourdan.

THREE COMRADES (1938) MGM. Screenplay by F. Scott Fitzgerald. Based on the novel by Erich Maria Remarque. Directed by Frank Borzage. Starring Robert Taylor, Margaret Sullavan, Franchot Tone, Robert Young.

THREE MUSKETEERS, THE (1948) MGM. Screenplay by Robert Ardrey, from the novel by Alexandre Dumas. Directed by George Sidney. Starring Lana Turner, Gene Kelly, June Allyson, Van Heflin.

TITANIC (1953) 20th. Screenplay by Charles Brackett, Walter Reisch, Richard Breen. Directed by Jean Negulesco. Starring Clifton Webb, Barbara Stanwyck, Robert Wagner.

TO BE OR NOT TO BE (1984) Brooksfilms. Screenplay by Thomas Meehan, Ronny Graham, from a film by Ernst Lubitsch. Directed by Alan Johnson. Starring Mel Brooks, Anne Bancroft, Charles Durning, Jose Ferrer.

TO CATCH A THIEF (1955) Par. Screenplay by

John Michael Hayes. Directed by Alfred Hitchcock. Starring Cary Grant, Grace Kelly, Jessie Royce Landis.

TO EACH HIS OWN (1946) Par. Screenplay by Charles Brackett, Jacques Thery. Directed by Mitchell Leisen. Starring Olivia de Havilland, John Lund.

TO HAVE AND HAVE NOT (1944) WB. Screenplay by Jules Furthman and William Faulkner. Based on the novel by Ernest Hemingway. Directed by Howard Hawks. Starring Humphrey Bogart, Lauren Bacall, Walter Brennan.

TOM JONES (1963) UA. Screenplay by John Osborne, from the novel by Henry Fielding. Directed by Tony Richardson. Starring Albert Finney, Susannah York.

TOP HAT (1935) RKO. Screenplay by Dwight Taylor and Allan Scott. Based on the musical by Dwight Taylor. Directed by Mark Sandrich. Starring Fred Astaire, Ginger Rogers, Edward Everett Horton.

TOPPER (1937) MGM. Screenplay by Jack Jerne, Eric Hatch, Eddie Moran, from the novel by Thorne Smith. Directed by Norman Z. McLeod. Starring Cary Grant, Roland Young, Constance Bennett.

TORRID ZONE (1940) WB. Screenplay by Richard Macaulay, Jerry Wald. Directed by William Keighley. Starring James Cagney, Pat O'Brien, Ann Sheridan.

TOUCH OF CLASS, A (1973) Avco. Screenplay by Melvin Frank, Jack Rose. Directed by Melvin Frank. Starring Glenda Jackson and George Segal.

TREASURE OF THE SIERRA MADRE, THE (1948) WB. Screenplay by John Huston. Based on the novel by B. Traven. Directed by John Huston. Starring Humphrey Bogart, Walter Huston, Tim Holt, Bruce Bennett.

TROUBLE IN PARADISE (1932) Par. Screenplay by Grover Jones, Samson Raphaelson, from the play by

Laszlo Aladar. Directed by Ernst Lubitsch. Starring Miriam Hopkins, Kay Francis, Herbert Marshall.

TRUE GRIT (1969) Par. Screenplay by Marguerite Roberts, from the novel by Charles Portis. Directed by Henry Hathaway. Starring John Wayne, Glen Campbell, Kim Darby.

TWENTIETH CENTURY (1934) Col. Screenplay by Ben Hecht and Charles MacArthur from their play. Directed by Howard Hawks. Starring John Barrymore, Carole Lombard.

2001: A SPACE ODYSSEY (1968) MGM. Screenplay by Stanley Kubrick and Arthur C. Clarke. Directed by Stanley Kubrick. Starring Keir Dullea, Gary Lockwood.

UNDER THE RAINBOW (1981) WB. Screenplay by Pat McCormick, Harry Kurnitz, Martin Smith. Directed by Steve Rash. Starring Chevy Chase, Carrie Fisher.

UNMARRIED WOMAN, AN (1978) 20th. Screenplay and directed by Paul Mazursky. Starring Jill Clayburgh, Alan Bates, Michael Murphy, Cliff Gorman.

VICTOR/VICTORIA (1983) MGM/UA. Screenplay by Blake Edwards. Based on a film written by Rheinhold Schuenzel. Directed by Blake Edwards. Starring Julie Andrews, James Garner, Robert Preston, Leslie Ann Warren.

VIRGINIAN, THE (1946) Par. Screenplay by Frances Goodrich and Albert Hackett. Directed by Stuart Gilmore. Starring Joel McCrea, Brian Donleavy.

VIVA ZAPATA! (1952) 20th. Screenplay by John Steinbeck. Directed by Elia Kazan. Starring Marlon Brando, Jean Peters, Anthony Quinn, Joseph Wiseman.

VOLTAIRE (1933) WB. Screenplay by Paul Green, Maude Howell, George Gibbs, Laurence Dudley. Starring George Arliss, Reginald Owen.

WAKE OF THE RED WITCH (1948) Rep. Screenplay by Harry Brown, from the novel by Garlan Roark. Directed by Edward Ludwig. Starring John Wayne, Gail Russell, Gig Young.

WARGAMES (1984) MGM/UA. Screenplay by Lawrence Lasker, Walter Parkes. Directed by John Badham. Starring Matthew Broderick, Dabney Coleman, Ally Sheedy.

WATCH ON THE RHINE (1943) WB. Screenplay by Dashiell Hammett, from the play by Lillian Hellman. Directed by Herman Shumlin. Starring Bette Davis, Paul Lukas, Geraldine Fitzgerald.

WAY OUT WEST (1937) MGM. Screenplay by Charles Rogers, Felix Adler, James Parrott. Directed by James Horne. Starring Stan Laurel and Oliver Hardy.

WAY WE WERE, THE (1973) Col. Screenplay by Arthur Laurents, based on his novel. Directed by Sydney Pollack. Starring Barbra Streisand, Robert Redford, Bradford Dillman.

WE'RE NO ANGELS (1990) Par. Screenplay by David Mamet. Directed by Neil Jordan. Starring Robert De Niro, Sean Penn, Demi Moore.

WESTERNER, THE (1940) UA. Screenplay by Jo Swerling, Niven Busch. Directed by William Wyler. Starring Gary Cooper, Walter Brennan.

WEST SIDE STORY (1961) UA. Screenplay by Ernest Lehman, based on the stage play by Arthur Laurents. Directed by Robert Wise, Jerome Robbins. Starring Natalie Wood, Richard Beymer.

WHAT'S UP, DOC? (1972) WB. Screenplay by Buck Henry, David Newman, Robert Benton. Directed by Peter Bogdanovich. Starring Barbra Streisand, Ryan O'Neal, Madeline Kahn.

WHERE'S POPPA? (1970) MGM/UA. Screenplay by

Robert Klane, based on his novel. Directed by Carl Reiner. Starring George Segal, Ruth Gordon, Ron Leibman.

WHICH WAY TO THE FRONT? (1970) WB. Screenplay by Gerald Gardner and Dee Caruso. Directed by Jerry Lewis. Starring Jerry Lewis, John Wood, Jan Murray.

WHITE CARGO (1942) MGM. Screenplay by Leon Gordon, based on his play. Directed by Richard Thorpe. Starring Hedy Lamarr, Walter Pidgeon, Richard Carlson.

WHITE HEAT (1949) WB. Screenplay by Ivan Goff, Ben Roberts. Directed by Raoul Walsh. Starring James Cagney and Virginia Mayo.

WHO FRAMED ROGER RABBIT (1988) Tou. Screenplay by Peter Seaman. Based on the novel by Gary Wolf. Directed by Robert Zemeckis. Starring Bob Hoskins, Christopher Lloyd.

WHO'S AFRAID OF VIRGINIA WOOLF? (1966) WB. Screenplay by Ernest Lehman, from the play by Edward Albee. Directed by Mike Nichols. Starring Elizabeth Taylor, Richard Burton, George Segal, Sandy Dennis.

WILD BUNCH, THE (1969) WB-7 Arts. Screenplay by Walon Green, Sam Peckinpaw. Directed by Sam Peckinpah. Starring William Holden, Ernest Borgnine, Robert Ryan.

WILD IN THE STREETS (1968) American International. Screenplay by Robert Thom. Directed by Barry Shear. Starring Christopher Jones, Shelley Winters, Hal Holbrook.

WILD ONES, THE (1954) Col. Screenplay by John Paxton. Directed by Laslo Benedek. Starring Marlon Brando, Lee Marvin, Mary Murphy.

WILL SUCCESS SPOIL ROCK HUNTER? (1957) 20th. Screenplay by Frank Tashlin, from the play by

George Axelrod. Directed by Frank Tashlin. Starring Jayne Mansfield, Tony Randall, Betsy Drake.

WIZARD OF OZ, THE (1939) MGM. Screenplay by Noel Langley, Florence Ryerson, Edgar Allan Wolff, from the book by L. Frank Baum. Directed by Victor Fleming. Starring Judy Garland, Frank Morgan, Ray Bolger, Bert Lahr, Jack Haley.

WOMAN NEXT DOOR, THE (1981) Les Films du Carrosse. Screenplay by François Truffaut, Suzanne Schiffman, Jean Aurel. Directed by François Truffaut. Starring Gerard Depardieu, Fanny Ardant.

WOMAN OF THE YEAR (1942) MGM. Screenplay by Ring Lardner and Michael Kanen. Directed by George Stevens. Starring Spencer Tracy and Katharine Hepburn.

WOMEN, THE (1939) MGM. Screenplay by Anita Loos, from the play by Clare Boothe. Directed by George Cukor. Starring Norma Shearer, Joan Crawford, Rosalind Russell, Paulette Goddard.

WORKING GIRL (1989) 20th. Screenplay by Kevin Wade. Directed by Mike Nichols. Starring Melanie Griffith, Harrison Ford, Sigourney Weaver.

WORLD'S GREATEST ATHLETE, THE (1973) Buena Vista. Screenplay by Gerald Gardner, Dee Caruso. Directed by Robert Scheer. Starring John Amos, Tim Conway, Jan Michael Vincent.

WUTHERING HEIGHTS (1939) UA. Screenplay by Ben Hecht, Charles MacArthur. Directed by William Wyler, from the novel by Emily Brontë. Starring Merle Oberon, Laurence Olivier, David Niven.

YANKEE DOODLE DANDY (1942) WB. Screenplay by Robert Buckner, Edmund Joseph. Directed by Michael Curtiz. Starring James Cagney, Joan Leslie, Walter Huston.

YEAR OF THE DRAGON (1986) MGM/UA.

Screenplay by Oliver Stone, Michael Cimino, from the novel by Alex Thomson. Directed by Michael Cimino. Starring Mickey Rourke, John Lone.

YOU CAN'T CHEAT AN HONEST MAN (1939) Univ. Screenplay by George Marion, Jr., Richard Mack, Everett Freeman. Directed by George Marshall and Edward Clive. Starring W.C. Fields.

YOUNG FRANKENSTEIN (1974) 20th. Screenplay by Gene Wilder and Mel Brooks. Directed by Mel Brooks. Starring Gene Wilder, Marty Feldman, Peter Boyle, Madeline Kahn.

YOUNG MR. LINCOLN (1939) 20th. Screenplay by Lamar Trotti. Directed by John Ford. Starring Henry Fonda, Alice Brady.

ZIEGFELD FOLLIES (1946) MGM. Directed by Vincente Minnelli. Starring Fred Astaire, Lucille Ball, Fanny Brice, Esther Williams, Judy Garland, Jimmy Durante.

ZORBA THE GREEK (1964) International Classics. Screenplay and directed by Michael Cocoyannis, from a novel by Nikos Kazantzakis. Starring Anthony Quinn, Alan Bates.

ZORRO, THE GAY BLADE (1981) Melvin Simon. Screenplay by Hal Dresner. Directed by Peter Medak. Starring George Hamilton, Lauren Hutton, Ron Leibman.

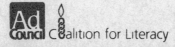